Handbook for the Amateur UFO Investigator

By Brian D. Parsons, PhD

Published by Lulu for BP Guy Productions™, Twinsburg, Ohio.

ISBN 978-1-387-08300-8

Dedication

This effort is dedicated to the research, life, and reach of Gaurav Tiwari. I miss you my friend.

Handbook for the Amateur UFO Investigator

Introduction

The UFO field is really the newest addition to the anomalous research family. Ghost stories have been told for thousands of years with one of the earliest documented firsthand accounts from Pliny the Younger nearly 2,000 years ago and the first documented ghost investigation in 1662 by Joseph Glanvill. Research into cryptids, such as the Loch Ness Monster and Bigfoot, began in the 1930s although research into other strange creatures had been going on for hundreds of years.

When I began my journey into investigating ghosts I did so with a skeptical eye. I learned about parapsychology and psychical research and how science was not in favor of the pursuit. It didn't take long for me to become a bit of a believer with some of the content and yet it didn't take me long after that to realize how quickly I lost my perspective. A few years into researching and investigating ghosts I decided to look at the other two areas of the anomalous world.

My peek into the world of UFOs was a bit skeptical and it started with buying and borrowing a few books from the bookstore and library respectively. Some may argue my statement that UFO research is the youngest since beliefs in life from other worlds has existed for hundreds of years as well, but this is where we need to separate UFOs and extraterrestrials.

Belief in UFOs is different than belief in ghosts or cryptids as it demands an absolute. You might believe in Bigfoot, but not Mothman and that's OK. You might feel that some types of ghosts don't exist or that many types of experiences are not what people think and that is OK. However, when it comes to believing in UFOs either you believe that extraterrestrials exist or they don't (how else would they get here?).

Yet, one important thing to remember is that a UFO means unidentified flying object and does not have to mean an alien flying around in a saucer although it is usually associated with that thought. If we identify the craft as being flown by aliens it is no longer unidentified and no longer a UFO! However, this belief is generally implied when discussing UFOs and the pursuit of this subject may demand a bit of belief in intelligent life being out there although it shouldn't be completely necessary.

As researchers and investigators we need to understand that there is a difference between an unidentified flying object and an alien flying around the skies in a flying saucer. A UFO by basic definition essentially means it is not immediately known by the observer. It is our job to solve that mystery and not to get caught up in the multitude of other things that seem to define UFO culture. I cannot deny the many other aspects of this culture and while I have attempted to keep the "political" aspects of ghosts and cryptids out of other volumes of my "handbook" series I feel it is a necessary evil to cover them in regards to UFOs as it plays a large part in the culture.

Like my other books I remind you that this is not the end-all be-all book for investigating this topic. This effort in your hands is a culmination of other works in which I reference as well as a guide to investigate UFO cases from my own experience as an anomalous researcher working with many other people over the years. However, there are a lot of other pieces that I cannot cover within this book that you should be aware of which will be mentioned as we move through this book. I did not want this book to become an overly technical "how to" book that explains everything since there are so many variations of things to look for to explain data and I don't want people to assume I've covered everything. But, I hope this books helps open a few minds and does help guide someone, hopefully you, to help solve a UFO case or twenty.

I had put off writing a handbook for the UFO researcher/investigator for years due to the fantastic resource of the *MUFON Field Investigator's Manual* from the Mutual UFO Network. I felt that this valuable resource should be the center of everyone that decides to investigate cases. However, with the cost of the binder as well as the scope I felt as if I could write a balanced look at this topic and provide a path for the average person to get into this field with a substantially lower cost and different focus. Obviously, the *MUFON Field Investigator's Manual* would serve as a valuable resource beyond this book.

Part I: I Know What I Saw

Chapter 1: Cultural Tracking: A Glance at UFO Sighting Reports

On June 24, 1947, Kenneth A. Arnold, a businessman and pilot, was flying his single engine aircraft near Mount Rainier in the state of Washington. Arnold was on his way to Yakima, Washington, but had planned to spend about an hour looking for a downed U.S. military transport aircraft that had been reported missing.

It was during this time that Arnold encountered a bright flash that he feared was another aircraft approaching him. He searched the sky around him quickly and only saw a DC-9 many miles away that could not have been the source. As he continued to scan the skies he suddenly saw another flash that came from what he could see was a line of 9 aircraft to his north.

He initially thought they might be geese, but with the altitude and obvious reflection he realized they were definitely aircraft. He then assumed these were military jets as they were positioned in an echelon, or diagonal, formation as they flew toward him. As the craft got closer he realized that something was not right as the craft were shaped differently than anything he had ever seen. The craft were shaped like wide crescents without a tail or cockpit. Watching the aircraft fly past him at astonishing speed he used known points as well as his clock to estimate that the craft were flying in excess of 1,700 miles per hour.

Arnold would tell some people about his sighting when he landed in Yakima, but he headed off to Oregon and would finally be interviewed on June 25th. During his interview he described the aircraft as "saucer shaped" or like a "pie plate" although would state they were crescent shaped years later. Arnold also described how the craft moved and stating, "…they flew like a saucer would if you skipped it across water." When the report hit the newspapers the term flying saucer was born and the modern area of strange aerial crafts began.

Kenneth Arnold was a very experienced pilot and had done many things during his experience to rule out reflections as well as determine their speed and size at a distance. The U.S. military determined his sighting to be either a mirage, reflection, or just a flock of geese despite his claims. However, on July 4, 1947, a United Airlines crew also spotted a group of 5 to 9 craft similar in description to Arnold's over Idaho as the plane headed to Seattle. Another similar sighting occurred on July 12, 1947, over Tulsa, Oklahoma.

While this story is widely considered the case that brought flying saucers, and eventually UFOs, to the forefront of the general public it is far from the earliest account of an unidentified flying object. It is, however, the beginning of the research and investigation era of UFOs since Arnold had measured and described the craft in intricate detail that had never been documented before. This case also opened the door for the U.S. military to begin investigating cases.

Another interesting takeaway from the Arnold case is the point that many of the "facts" of the sighting are varying and even contradictory in various resources that discuss the sighting. If Kenneth Arnold presented only the facts as he experienced them back in 1947 why is it that the information has been dissolved in different ways? One of the major reasons for this is the fact that this story has been told and retold so many times. One would think that a field with so many researchers who want the truth to be known that we could at least get the facts straight about one of the most prolific sightings in history.

This is one of the driving forces behind this book and why we need more researchers who wish to document history rather than rewrite and profit from it. I know, silly that I'm writing a book and saying this, but you will find that the effort behind this book isn't to convince you that these stories are real or that flying saucers, UFOs, or even aliens actually exist. I'm here to help provide the foundation for you to get out there and determine that. To do this we must learn to leave our opinions and beliefs behind and focus on the work that we intend to do. The bottom line is to not view these incidents as proving that intelligent alien life exists and are flying through our atmosphere in sophisticated flying machines. No, rather we should simply focus on explaining what the person saw plain and simple. Solving the mystery is the most important thing and the facts should take us to the solution and our emotions, beliefs, and expectations should not interfere.

One of the earliest purported UFO sightings comes from ancient Egypt. On or around 1440 BC, Thutmose III, the sixth Pharaoh of the Eighteenth Dynasty, had described fiery discs in the sky which was recorded by his scribes in what is referred to as the Tulli Papyrus. Alberto Tulli is said to have come across the papyrus while visiting Cairo in 1933. However, the claims of this sighting are highly questionable as the information Tulli had in his possession was not the original papyrus and the information presented has been questioned by many scholars over the years. Many feel that the information is meaningless since there is little or no evidence that the Tulli Papyrus ever existed at all. However, the Tulli Papyrus continues to be a log in the fire of belief for many UFO believers.

The ancient Greeks and Romans also documented many sightings that have been described as torches in the sky, great chariots with soldiers, and other descriptions of UFOs. However, many of these accounts are more than likely bolides (exploding meteorites) or other natural phenomena. While there are a few accounts that seem to defy logic there is really little information other than vague descriptions that unfortunately do not help credibility for the existence of UFOs or offer any clues to attach ancient sightings to current ones.

Frustrating, right?

As we move forward into the 19th century we begin to hear stories of giant airships. One of the most popular stories of this timeframe is right at the end of the century and is that of the Aurora, Texas, airship crash. On, or around, April 17, 1897, an airship is said to have crashed into the windmill of Judge J.S. Proctor as reported two days after by the *Dallas Morning News* with Aurora writer resident S.E. Haydon.

The appearance and subsequent crash of the airship and destruction of the windmill was described in the story, but it wasn't the most impressive part of it. Apparently, with the crash an occupant of the airship was killed and was subsequently buried in the local graveyard. A historical marker from the Texas Historical Commission marks the Aurora Cemetery retelling the event. This occupant is described as being a Martian (not sure how that could be determined) and has been the center of controversy and investigation on a small handful of UFO based television shows.

One longstanding argument in favor of the Aurora crash is that the airplane did not take flight until 1903. While this is true it should be noted that airships had been flying since 1785 and were being developed heavily in the 1880s. This serves as an important clue for several topics that we will cover in this book.

While this story received a lot of attention from 2005's *UFO Files* television show as well as 2008's *UFO Hunters*, it has never been seen as more than a legend by many even in the UFO field.

Former Aurora mayor, Barbara Brammer, provided the show *UFO Files* with information that she felt explained the UFO sighting as an elaborate hoax. She stated a number of events that occurred with the town just prior to the event that seemed to make the sighting a way to keep the town from drying up. S.E. Haydon, the author of the story, was known as a jokester of his time and despite the conspiracy theories about a missing headstone and metallic objects from the graveyard to purportedly strange objects found at the bottom of Proctor's old well the story seems to be more of a legend than anything. Even the sign outside of the cemetery erected by the state of Texas which describes various historical references tied to the graveyard says that it's a legend.

Moving back into the 1940s we see some interesting diversity in stories. On February 24, 1942, the incident known as the Battle of Los Angeles or also known as the Great Los Angeles Air Raid took place. The United States had just entered World War II and it was less than three months since the attack on Pearl Harbor. Air raid sirens prompted a citywide blackout. The 37th Coast Artillery Brigade suddenly began firing anti-aircraft shells from 3:16 AM to 4:14 AM on February 24th at purported aircraft. While no aircraft were reported on radar or shot down over 1,400 shells were fired into the air along with .50 caliber machine guns. Amazingly, no one was killed by the shells or machine guns, but five people did die from car accidents and heart attacks combined as a result of the event.

While many attributed this reaction to nerves and fear many felt that this was the result of the sighting of UFOs. Some believe that the famous photographs of the searchlights clearly show UFOs in the sky. The lights, however, are more than likely the explosions of the shells which some reportedly mistook for aircraft during the event. The photograph was also manipulated prior to being printed in numerous newspapers. It is popularly believed that a weather balloon was the catalyst for the air raid sirens which ultimately lead to the firing of the guns. In 2011, Columbia Pictures released the movie "*Battle: Los Angeles*" based on the story, however, this fictional portrayal included a crippling alien attack set in modern times.

One of the more interesting and potentially convincing UFO sightings involves the Foo Fighters. No, not the rock band, but the interesting bright spheres that the band was named after. In 1944 the 415th Night Fighter Squadron of the United States Air Force encountered bright orange and red fireballs that they could not outmaneuver. Even at speeds of 200 miles per hour the eight to 10 balls seemed to play with the aircraft. Radar operator Donald J. Meiers, who witnessed the strange lights, is said to have slammed down a copy of *Smokey Stover* comics (which frequently used the word "Foo") during his debriefing and proclaiming it to be just another "Foo Fighter", although he used another colorful "F" word prior to that (Lindell 1991).

These strange fireballs would be seen by numerous other pilots while fighting in WWII. For some it was thought that this was a secret Nazi weapon of some sort. Others felt there was a natural explanation such as electrical discharge from the aircraft through the wingtips or even ball lightning as well as the concept of "aviator's vertigo" which suggests a hallucination despite photographs being taken of the glowing orbs. Interestingly, German and Japanese pilots also described the glowing spheres and Axis powers also feared that the Allies had created a new super weapon. What exactly the Foo Fighters were still remains a mystery today.

Of course, also in the 1940s, we have the currently most famous UFO case from Roswell, but we'll examine this case in a subsequent chapter. The 1940s and 1950s were full of many interesting UFO stories that would easily fill any book but I'll only mention a few more. As we've seen so far some of these more prominent sightings occurred to those involved with the military. One would think that these sightings would have more credibility or could help validate these sightings but despite the mounting cases that does not appear to be the case.

One interesting case from government witnesses comes from popular case involving United States and United Kingdom military personnel of the same craft. This incident, known as the Bentwaters incident or Lakenheath-Bentwaters incident, occurred in England on August 13 and 14, 1956, and was documented in the U.S. Air Force's Project Blue Book. The United States had occupied the Bentwaters base from 1951 through 1993 and the base is currently inactive.

The incident began at 9:30 PM local time when the radar at the Bentwaters facility began tracking a high speed object. Another group of targets was also located on radar and were traveling slower than the initial object. A trainer jet was asked to attempt visual contact with any of the objects, but reported a bright object which was later determined to be the planet Mars.

Bentwaters then tracked another super high speed object, in excess of 2,000 miles per hour, approaching the base. An observer on the ground as well as one in an airplane both observed a rapidly moving white light moving over the base. As the radar object moved away Bentwaters contacted RAF Lakenheath to be on the lookout for the radar targets.

The base was able to track the incoming targets and personnel witnessed several objects make impossible maneuvers over the base before disappearing. It was also reported that fighters were scrambled to attempt to intercept the radar target. When they found the object one pilot was able to lock his radar on it which meant it was truly a solid object. However, the object then closely followed the aircraft despite the pilot's attempt at shaking it off his tail for several tense minutes (Perkins 1968).

Another interesting sighting occurred in Phoenix, Arizona, in 1996 and was witnessed by thousands of people from the border of Nevada through Phoenix to the edge of Tucson. The incident occurred on March 13, 1997, and began as hundreds of people began reporting seeing a large V or triangular shaped lights moving across the state. At the same time residents in Phoenix began to report to local authorities a gathering of lights in the sky over the city.

These lights got all of the attention, and still do, when it comes to the Phoenix Lights story. There were many videos shot of the lights over Phoenix despite the technology being nothing compared to today. This was a time a year removed from cell phone cameras and before DVD camcorders flooded the market so what we have is multiple VHS cassette recordings of the lights.

As you may well know, the hovering lights over Phoenix have been primarily explained as flares dropped by aircraft from the Barry Goldwater Range at Luke Air Force Base. These flares would be explainable from the wind direction as well as from the perspective of those that captured them on video or film. However, the initial sighting is still a bit more of a heated debate.

Some feel that the large solid object was in fact a group of airplanes. It has been suggested that a group of Air National Guard jets had been flying in a V formation from Luke Air Force Base and may have fooled people due to being grouped together. Despite this, the Phoenix Lights have become one of the greatest UFO mysteries in recent years. To some, the latter formation of flares over Phoenix served as a trick to fool people into not focusing on the initial event of a large craft moving over the whole state.

Dr. Lynne D. Kitei, M.D. was able to get video footage of the Phoenix lights on March 13, 1997. But she had also claimed to have seen similar lights near her home in Phoenix for a few years and despite her and her husband being scientists and skeptics towards UFOs their experiences convinced them that there is something going on in our skies. Do her miraculous and ongoing experiences with the lights in the sky validate what the thousands of others saw that night? We may never know, but Kitei's book is worth the read if you have an interest in the Phoenix Lights.

The previous examples are, of course, merely a sample of the large amounts of UFO cases turned in year after year. These highlighted in this chapter are just merely sightings and do not take into consideration other types of UFO phenomena such as close encounters, crashes, or other types of strange phenomena such as the Bigfoot-UFO flap of 1973-1974 in southwest Pennsylvania as researched by Stan Gordon.

It's easy to get lost in all of these reports and quickly become a believer in UFOs being a creation of some advanced civilization. Again, we must remind ourselves that UFO stands for Unidentified Flying Object and does not imply an alien created or driven craft. This merely means that at the time of the report the object was unknown and does not mean that an explanation will never be determined.

As we have seen with some of the previous examples, others we may cover in this book, and ones you may encounter elsewhere there are a plethora of potential explanations. Further in this book we will explore one of the more problematic explanations of the hoax. We will also explore misinterpretations from a physical as well as a psychological point of view.

In stepping back from the individual reports we see that despite so many seemingly credible reports there are very few that really defy a logical solution. That's not to say that all UFO sightings lack a logical explanation or that all logical explanations can verify the object seen. The key here is that we must be careful not to lump all of these stories together to provide validation for our opinions, assumptions, or beliefs behind UFO sightings.

Another startling assumption we should also consider is the potential fact that UFOs in the context of being created by aliens may not be real at all. Why would someone who is writing a book on how to investigate UFOs say this in the first chapter of his book? Well, first I think it's fair to throw this out here now instead of the last chapter! In all seriousness, the job of anyone investigating anything is to find answers not to suit their personal beliefs or even to attempt to validate an experience for a client.

We should be well aware of the potential that any case that has ever come up dealing with UFOs might just have a logical explanation to it other than a craft traveling light years to just snoop. Granted, the scope of this book is not to speculate such things but it should be something that the reader speculates on his or her own. This book will explore many potential explanations for

UFOs that are rational and logical. The other side of the coin, is obviously, that you will not find an explanation and the sighting will go down as truly an unidentified flying object. My goal here in this book is to provide you with enough insight that you will be able to cover a fair amount of potential logical solutions, but there may be plenty more not covered in these pages.

Again, if we step back and look at UFO reports through just basic sighting information and descriptions we might just see a startling pattern. When looking back at the ancient cases we see descriptions that seem to be much different than how UFOs are described in modern times. The Greeks and Romans described large chariots or even sailing ships in the sky with soldiers carrying weapons similar to what was in use in Europe at the time. We have seen UFO shapes morph over time from flying discs to triangles and orbs. Could it be that our vision of UFOs is influenced by our culture?

Beyond culture there are also the individuals who report these sightings. Cigar shaped objects were often seen in the skies in the late 1800s, as this was the technology of the time as airship technology was booming. During World War I and World War II these sightings were construed as pieces of advanced military technology. To those who live with Catholic beliefs in various times these sightings are the act of God (Goode). These individual beliefs are heavily influenced by the culture of the time and as we break down the times and varied belief we see the reflection of that belief in the types of UFO experiences that occur.

Cultural tracking refers to how UFOs tend to reflect the culture and technology in the timeframe in which they appear (Spencer 1991). Kenneth Arnold's UFO sighting was crescent shaped, but was labeled by the media as a flying saucer. Arnold had meant that the craft moved "like a saucer would if you skipped it across the water", but the media liked the label and it stuck. Shortly after the headlines and popular use of the term flying saucer people began to describe seeing the popular shape in the skies.

We have seen these changes occur even with events such as the Phoenix Lights. After the Phoenix Lights story broke out in 1997 triangle shaped UFOs became very popular. One could even argue that the television show *The X-Files*, which began in September of 1993 and was an extremely popular show, might have had an effect on the Phoenix Lights as the show featured triangular shaped craft multiple times through its run.

Of course, the explanation could be that since people have a current thought of culture they would react to something strange in the sky by describing it as they would know best. Ancient Greeks would know nothing of a cigar or blimp shaped craft and they would describe the things they saw in the sky based on what they knew of the world around them (Nicholson 2013). This might satisfy the explanation of describing shapes in the sky, but those who have described seeing aliens have also changed their descriptions as the times and cultures have changed. We have seen early reports from "little green men" morph into our current concept of "grays" and have passed through many changes over the years due to the culture surrounding aliens (Nickell 2001).

Regardless, we should study the cases of the past if for nothing else their reflection of the culture of UFO belief. While many of these are significant cases within the UFO field we should not allow any one or any collection of cases define it. Each case should be approached as a separate event unless it occurs within the same time frame and flight path and has not been affected by social media or other methods of instant communication.

Your mission as a UFO researcher is to maintain a balanced approach in reviewing a case. The approach should not be one of attempting to validate the witnesses' claim or to debunk the sighting, just to get the facts straight. Your mission as a UFO investigator is to attempt to identify what has so far been unidentified.

Chapter 2: Ancient Assumptions

One of the areas I managed to avoid to a degree in previous technical manuals on ghosts and cryptozoology was the politics behind those subjects. The what, when, where, and why were left out in order to focus on the how. I focused on the subjects at hand and attempted to keep the reader and potential researcher/investigator focused on the goal of the investigation instead. The subject of UFOs, as mentioned already, is a bit of a different monster. The culture of belief has become entrenched with roots of belief systems that can affect how people interpret UFOs and their purpose if they do exist.

One area of concern for UFOs is the idea that alien cultures have already been to Earth and have woven their way into humankind and have impacted cultures or have even potentially created us in their own vision. There are many thoughts about ancient aliens and it's not the purpose of this book to speculate on theories of this field as a whole or in ones such as this that have no bearing on investigating. There are plenty of other resources for examining whether this is true or not. However, I felt it necessary to discuss the ancient alien (or ancient astronaut) theories since it seems to have become quite the distraction in the last few years toward the field as a whole and yet a growing part of the culture.

The television show *Ancient Aliens* made its debut on the History Channel with a pilot episode in March, 2009, with the first season beginning in April of 2010. The show has eleven seasons in the can so far finishing in September of 2016. The ratings for the show have held steady and many people, since the show began, have taken much of what the show has said as potential fact or at least highly likely to have occurred. I mean, it's the History Channel!

Unfortunately, most historians and scientists disagree and call the show "farfetched" and full of pseudoscience and pseudohistory. Personally, I have never really been a fan of the show and reacted to the few episodes I did watch the same way I reacted to *Ghost Hunters* and *Ghost Adventurers* when I watched those programs as well (that involved a lot of arguing and pointing at the television). However, while I'm not a fan of the ancient alien or ancient astronaut theories I expected a little more from the History Channel than what was provided as even someone who has a little more than a casual interest in history found many glaring issues with the few episodes I did watch.

The show has rustled the feathers of many scientists, historians, anthropologists, archaeologists, and even paleontologists. The Ancient Aliens show once asserted that dinosaurs were sent to extinction by aliens so that humans could exist. The show misrepresented facts such as carbon-14 dating not being reliable. No kidding, paleontologists use radiometric techniques to date fossils as carbon-14 only works for carbon based materials up to 60,000 years old (Switek 2012).

That particular episode they also suggested that Ica Stones that depicted dinosaurs were proof positive that men and dinosaurs existed together. The Ica Stones are more than likely hoaxes and many have admitted to selling hoaxed stones. That same episode featured many creationist views yet used science to explain other aspects to support their beliefs even though many claims went against other things said during the show. Like many episodes of the show so many inaccurate things were portrayed just to wow the viewer and the show has gone on to continue to contradict itself about multiple things that were said previously even during the same episode.

The entire series is essentially based on books written by Erich von Däniken, who makes several appearances in the series. Däniken's first and best selling release, *Chariots of the Gods?*, he set forth the notion that early man was not knowledgeable enough to construct monuments like Stonehenge, the Egyptian pyramids, and other achievements due to limited knowledge or tools. Many claims made in this and subsequent books have been attacked by scholars, historians, and other true experts in various fields where Däniken makes false claims with no resources to back them up or makes his opinions into facts. He's even asserted that the banana was brought to Earth by aliens in his book, yet revealed that he made it up to help sell books (Mori).

King Pacal's sarcophagus lid with figure

Interestingly, the ancient alien hypothesis was first thought of by a Russian mathematician. Matest M. Agrest published some interesting work in 1959 that would become part of the fabric of ancient alien mythology. His work, and the fictional work of H.P. Lovecraft, influenced Louis Pauwels and Jacques Bergier to write *The Morning of the Magicians* in 1960. This book ultimately influenced many in the west including Erich von Däniken (Colavito).

One of the centerpieces of the ancient alien/astronaut claim is the sarcophagus lid from King Pacal's tomb. This 7' wide and 12' long stone lid that weighs several tons was put into place around 680 A.D. *Ancient Aliens* asserts that the lid depicts King Pacal flying a rocket into space. During the episode that discusses the sarcophagus lid Däniken states, "You see his upper hand – he is manipulating some controls. From the lower hand – he is turning something on. The heel of his left foot is on a kind of pedal and, outside the capsule, you see a linking flame. This is incredible. This is absolute proof of extraterrestrials."

Archaeologists believe that the artwork depicts King Pacal's journey to the afterlife shortly following his death. The symbols displayed on the lid are universal in Mayan culture and appear in many works through time. While no other Mayan artwork depict going into space the final nail in the coffin should be that the artwork is on the lid of King Pacal's tomb. This fact pretty much goes with the symbolism of traveling to the afterlife and doesn't make sense of being a space traveler. Not to mention that if this was a spacecraft it is poorly designed. This is an example of what I previously mentioned of inserting our current culture into things that we are observing. In this case, it's not creating UFOs in shapes that we expect but carving past history based on our current ideas of what a person would be doing if seated on their back pointing upward (preparing for liftoff in a rocket).

The Crucifixion (1350)

Some may point to the fact that UFOs were depicted in artwork during the middle ages. One popular painting, *The Crucifixion* painted in 1350, is said to contain not one but two UFOs that are purportedly chasing each other. If you think in terms of this being a UFO then it does make visual sense. Other paintings show similar UFO shapes above the crucifixion of Jesus so it has to be –aliens.

The reality is this was a piece of symbolism that was placed in every painting in the medieval period and was started by the

Romans. The sun and moon are depicted in these paintings as being witnesses to the crucifixion of Christ and are usually facing the cross (Cuoghi). It seems the producers of the show chose artwork that seems to display a UFO instead of the dozens of other interpretations which are much more obvious to what is occurring.

Madonna with Child with the Infant St. John the Baptist

Another hot topic for UFOs that are purportedly in paintings is ones that appear with Madonna. In the painting, *Madonna with Child with the Infant St. John the Baptist*, we see what appears to be a UFO hovering over the shoulder of Madonna. We also see that a man is witnessing this event and has his hand shading his eyes. Also, his dog is also witnessing this unidentified flying object hovering close by.

Well, that's what the ancient alien theorists would have you believe. In reality, this was again symbolism by artists in the medieval time period depicting a religious scene. The object that is supposedly a UFO is actually depicting a passage in the bible that relates to the birth of Christ. The shepherd seen in the painting refers to the verse as well which mentions shepherds which have been similarly depicted in many other paintings that reflect the gospel of Luke and the birth of Jesus. A quick examination of similar art of the period clearly depicts the very similar imagery, but not quite as dramatic of a UFO scene as the work depicted during the show or peddled by ancient alien theorists. The lack of understanding cultural symbolism in paintings does not stop there either.

The painting, *The Annunciation with Saint Emidius*, is said to have a large UFO in the sky shooting a laser beam toward Mary. This, again, is symbolism in numerous paintings throughout history. The UFO is actually a cloud with a pair of circles of angels which is depicted in numerous other paintings. The beam of light symbolizes the Holy Spirit which impregnates Mary. Again, this is a very common theme that also includes a dove which is displayed in numerous other paintings. Ancient alien theorists tend to choose the paintings that are the most ambiguous in showing these symbols which would relay more of their spiritual meaning instead of a mysterious spacecraft and other "out of this world" details.

The Annunciation with Saint Emidius (1486)

The reality is that *Ancient Aliens* has depicted a lot about alien culture that simply is not true or is created purely out of belief. These are just the tip of the iceberg when it comes to the current 119 episodes that have appeared on television to date. I could go on and on from episode to episode, but hopefully you get the gist of this chapter.

One would have to use some common sense and basic logic when watching this show to realize there are some major gaps in the basic premise that aliens once influenced humans. If aliens were such a major influence then why are there not more clues to their interaction with humans? Why would there only be subtle hints of UFOs in paintings or with sculptures if there was such a major influence from these beings? If, in fact, aliens had influenced cultures numerous times through the ages one would think that there would not only be more clues to their past interaction with physical objects but also with writings, mentions in stories, drawings, and numerous other homages to their otherworldly assistance in guiding us to the next step in evolution.

One would also think that if they did help build ancient monuments that they would be a little bit better than what we see here on Earth. I mean, they would have built spaceships to travel across the galaxy and while the Egyptian pyramids are impressive I would hope alien technology would be a little better than that. Granted, ancient alien theorists point out that all they had to work with were Earth materials which hindered their greatness. I'm not wholly opposed to the ancient alien hypothesis, but there would have to be much better evidence to support these ideas than even what *Ancient Aliens* has provided.

The big issue here is that the work of Däniken has influenced the thought of ancient alien theories which lead to this popular television show. The show, *Ancient Aliens*, in turn has created a new generation of believers in the show and the concept that aliens have been here before or have created humans or allowed them to flourish since things are presented as fact even though they are mere opinion or blatantly wrong. We have to remember that just because people believe in something it does not make it true.

I do think that many people realize this show is wrong, but it has influenced the culture of belief toward UFOs just as the television show *Ghost Hunters* has in the way that ghost investigations are "supposed" to be conducted. This television show alone has altered how people interpret alien life which also affects belief in UFOs zipping around the Earth. It spews so much misinformation mixed in with a small amount of truth that the viewer honestly doesn't know what is real and what isn't until it is pointed out to them piece by piece.

Other television shows have also spread misinformation such as the previously mentioned *UFO Hunters* and *UFO Files*. But, these shows also influenced people to question what they see in the skies and have brought people into the research and investigation arena. While these shows have also speculated about things I feel they have positively affected the culture of UFOs more so than the show *Ancient Aliens*. There are also a vast number of other television shows and movies that have done the same, but we will explore these in a subsequent chapter.

To learn more about how *Ancient Aliens* has inaccurately portrayed history, archeology, and artwork I highly recommend watching the YouTube video *Ancient Aliens Debunked*. The 3 hour video can be watched online at http://ancientaliensdebunked.com for free. The show is produced by Chris White and has commentary by Dr. Michael Heiser and contains numerous resources that actually back up the historical claims that are misrepresented in the *Ancient Aliens* television show.

Chapter 3: Deny Everything: Crash Cover-ups and Confusion

Friday, July 4, 1947, a late night summer thunderstorm was rolling through the high plains just outside of Roswell, New Mexico. Army Sgt. Frank Kaufmann, stationed at the Roswell Army Air Field, observed a radar target become very bright and then suddenly disappear from his screen. At the same time locals heard a strange boom between the late night thunder that sounded like an explosion and some even witness something fall from the sky.

The military had been on high alert since Tuesday, July 1, 1947, as Alamogordo, White Sands, and Roswell bases had tracked high speed targets on their radars which had not stopped until the mysterious disappearance that Friday night. The military quickly scrambled into action and sent out a team to investigate the potential crash area. It doesn't take them too long to locate the crash site where the object seemed to be wedged into the ground.

The object appeared to be nothing of this world and as the team got closer they noticed bodies strewn throughout the crash site. One body seems to be stuck near a gash in the side of the craft. Suddenly, a small being begins running away from the site. Stunned, one of the officers begins firing his weapon killing the person. Still a bit dazed from what is occurring they realize upon closer inspection the body looks to belong to a small grayish alien.

Over the next few days numerous events occurred in the desert near Roswell dealing with a second crash of an alien craft. William (Mac) Brazel discovers debris as he tends his cattle at the Foster Ranch on Saturday, July 5. By Monday, July 7, the military reaches the debris area after Brazel contacted the local sheriff who, in turn, contacted the military. Some of the debris is confiscated and the remaining pieces guarded.

 In the early morning hours of Tuesday, July 8, 1947, the media gets word from the military that a flying disc has been recovered and the story gets national attention. However, in just a matter of hours after making this proclamation the statement that a UFO was recovered was retracted by the Army. They now state that they were not able to immediately identify what was actually a weather balloon. The media accepts the answer and life in Roswell returns to normal.

This is just an example of a condensed account of one of the many versions told by many witnesses and purported military whistleblowers who came forward many years after the event. Despite what many think the "Roswell Incident" was not a major story when it happened and did not reshape how people viewed UFOs or government cover-ups. The story sounds like it is straight out of a movie or is possibly what movies are made of, but did it really happen?

With so many witnesses one would think that the story could be pieced back together and a seamless timeline of events could be established. This timeline could assist UFO researchers put the puzzle together to find out the truth about what happened in the New Mexico desert back in 1947. One such witness would be the operator of the radar at the Roswell Army Air Field, Sgt. Frank Kaufmann. Kaufmann was one of many people who claimed to have access to information about the "Roswell Incident" who came forward and his account is portrayed in the story that leads off this chapter. In it are some of his observations including the target disappearing on the radar screen to the gray alien being shot.

The big issue here is that Sgt. Frank Kaufmann was not who he says he was (Randle 2002). His credibility was questioned by many researchers and documents he produced from his military record to other purported secret government documents were ultimately found to be fabricated. Frank Kaufmann passed away in February of 2001. While fulfilling the wishes of Frank's wife, Juanita, Dr. Mark Rodeghier, of the Center for UFO Studies, Mark Chesney, and Don Schmitt, discovered that the documents that Kaufmann had produced were forged with old paper stock and old typewriters (Randle 2007). It seemed he had fooled many people into thinking his part was far greater than what it had been and his testimony became worthless.

The Roswell story was not considered eventful until well-known nuclear physicist and UFO researcher Stanton Friedman came across Major Jesse Marcel in 1978 by chance. Slowly, other researchers began to assist in unraveling the Roswell case to try and determine just what happened out there. Once Friedman and the others began to conduct research on the case it slowly began to become the phenomenal story it is known as today. In 1980, the *National Inquirer* ran a story on the Roswell UFO crash and suddenly it became a household name. Unfortunately, along the way it was becoming a very hot topic and a lot of people wanted to insert themselves into the story and then bask in the limelight that went with it.

As more names and faces came forward the story began to grow larger. It grew from one crashed craft to two. It went from alien writing to actual aliens that lead to secret testing, and alien autopsies. Some supposed "new" evidence would periodically be discovered or old evidence reanalyzed, deathbed confessions, and the Roswell saga even lead to the popularity of Area 51.

The information gathered from researching Roswell has been sketchy at best. Not much in the way of information has held up over time through careful research and many details change from purported witness to purported witness and even information from a single person seems to evolve over time. Remember the thunderstorm that lead off this chapter? It never happened.

In his book, *Roswell: Inconvenient Facts and the Will to Believe*, Karl T. Pflock states there were no thunderstorms in the region of southwest or southcentral New Mexico from July 2 to July 7. This information was verified by the National Weather Service and pretty much dampens (or dries up?) a number of variations of the Roswell story as told by a cast of characters.

The truth is there really was a crash in the desert in New Mexico in July of 1947. Many witnesses to the event tell the same story which has been corroborated with facts and research. While many scoff at the notion that the military stated it was a weather balloon it might be the only fact to be backed up in all of the hundreds of witnesses who have come forward about witnessing the crash or having inside information. Weather balloons, swamp gas, and other explanations have become a running joke to those who believe in UFOs, but as far as the "Roswell Incident" goes a weather balloon was determined to be the source not once, but twice.

Obviously, the initial reaction of a space disc was quickly retracted by the military back in 1947 within hours of making the claim. Many people cling to this mistake as proof positive that they were covering up information. Which in fact they were, that's right, the government admitted that the weather balloon explanation was indeed a cover-up (Appleyard).

In 1994, the Air Force created a 1,000 page report of memos and correspondence (*The Roswell Report: Fact vs. Fiction in the New Mexico Desert*) essentially stating that the debris was more than likely that of a crashed Project Mogul balloon. The balloon utilized sound equipment that was attempting to detect sound waves high in the atmosphere from Soviet nuclear bomb tests. The Mogul balloon was successful in detecting U.S. nuclear testing 6,000 miles away. This explanation was obviously not used to explain the Roswell incident due to it being a top secret project. Charles B. Moore launched a Project Mogul balloon in June of 1947 which subsequently crashed in the New Mexico desert in early July. Moore recognized the balloon in photographs of the "Roswell Incident" when it became a media sensation in the 1990s (Hedges).

A subsequent study released in 1997 discussed some of the details that some witnesses had described over the years of the purported Roswell crash. In *The Roswell Report: Case Closed*, Captain James McAndrew tackled many of the details that witnesses claimed were alien bodies or crashed UFOs. This information was not covered in the 1994 report. In this report many details of not only the physical evidence of misidentification but the incidents regarding the researchers creating ripe conditions for the fraudulent gathering of false witnesses were detailed. The report did a fantastic job of connecting actual known facts to the memories created by the dozens of purported witnesses and the patchwork of details outlined by the UFO researchers.

Authors seek UFO witnesses

Co-authors of a major book on the 1947 crash of at least one alien spacecraft in the New Mexico desert will be at the Golden Manor Motel in Socorro on Monday, Nov. 16 to seek out additional witnesses to these events.

Nuclear physicist Stanton T. Friedman and aviation/science writer Don Berliner, whose "Crash at Corona" is now in its second printing, want to meet with people having knowledge of the 1947 crashes.

Their book, being published in August by Paragon House of New York, is being prepared for a made-for-TV movie. It is the story of the discovery, retrieval, shipping and cover-up of what the authors call the most important scientific discovery of the past thousand years.

It is based on dozens of interviews with first- and second-hand civilian and ex-military witnesses to various parts of what is referred to as a very complex series of events.

In order to strengthen their case for government knowledge of what they call "the truth behind almost 50 years of UFO sightings," the authors are seeking out additional, reliable witnesses. It remains their policy to honor requests to keep the names of witnesses private.

For more information, contact Don Berliner, 1202 S. Washington St., Alexandria, VA., 22314 (703-548-0405); or Stanton T. Friedman, 79 Pembroke Crescent, Fredericton, New Brunswick E3B 2V1, Canada (506 457-0232).

Witnesses are invited to call either author collect or to make arrangements to meet them at any of their stops in New Mexico, which include the cities of Santa Fe, Albuquerque, Las Cruces, Alamogordo and Roswell.

November 4, 1992 *El Defensor Chieftain* (Socorro, N.M.)

When it's all said and done the "Roswell Incident" looks a lot like a bit of misidentification mixed with a lot of potential for cashing in on a good story. It has essentially evolved from an interesting story of a weather balloon to a complete mythology of government conspiracies, hushed witnesses, alien bodies, hidden spacecraft, and a plethora of information that inundates anyone who attempts to sort fact from fiction. The Roswell crash might be the most well-known UFO crash story in the United States but it certainly isn't the only one. In fact, it's not even the only popular one to have occurred in the state of New Mexico.

Aztec, New Mexico, is located in the northwest area of New Mexico about 60 miles east of the Four Corners area where New Mexico, Arizona, Utah, and Colorado all come together. The Aztec

UFO case is very similar to the "Roswell Incident" in the purported fact that a UFO supposedly crashed, the government responded, and then officials covered up the whole incident. A few different pieces of this case were that the craft that was recovered was found to be in one piece compared to the craft that was destroyed in a crash in Roswell. The incident, which occurred in February or March of 1948 (depending upon the source), was also said to have led to the collection of sixteen alien bodies that were alleged to be humanlike.

The saga of the Aztec UFO crash began in 1949 when Frank Scully, one of a few purported sources for the character name Dana Scully of X-Files fame, wrote a pair of articles that were said to document the findings of a scientist who had investigated the crash. Scully's interest and coverage of this story lead to a book, *Behind the Flying Saucers*, which was published in 1950.

Scully had been contacted by a friend of his, Silas M. Newton, who promised Scully the story of his life. Newton had a confidential informant, Leo GeBauer (whose confidential name was "Dr. Gee"), that could prove the thrilling story of a UFO crash and body retrieval as true. Not only this, but GeBauer had been able to reverse engineer some magnetic technology from the spacecraft that could help find oil underground among many other fantastic things.

This "doodlebug" as it was called, would help Newton discover oil. Newton had claimed to be a person of some regard in the oil industry. He used the popularity of Scully's articles and subsequent books to use this mystifying device to help locate oil through many interested investors.

Another journalist, J.P. Cahn, of the *San Francisco Chronicle* began conducting background research on the book and the statements made by Scully and Newton. In the end the "doodlebug" was nothing more than a disguised radio and the pair had concocted the entire UFO story just to get attention for the piece of equipment just to con some people out of money. Newton and Debauer were arrested on October 14, 1952, and tried on November 10, 1965. The pair were found guilty on fraud and conspiracy charges and sentenced to prison (Radford).

This story, as it turns out, was created as a mere elaborate con game that unfortunately ruined the career of Frank Scully. This crash story also disappeared from the minds of UFO researchers until it too was resurrected in the 1970s just like Roswell was. Many researchers point to the Aztec UFO case as being a clever cover-up by the U.S. government and seemingly ignore the fact it was created by two con men to separate people from their money. Perhaps that con still continues or it is possible that this story lumped into other ones such as Roswell might seemingly add to the credibility of the whole. Either way, the Aztec UFO story has no business as anything credible in the UFO research world based on the actual facts.

While I have read quite a few articles and books that made mention of this specific case the best information I have found by far comes from the book, *Mysterious New Mexico*, in the chapter, "The Great Aztec UFO Crash", by Benjamin Radford. Radford lives in New Mexico and has deeply researched this story for the true facts and has put together multiple resources on this topic.

Another interesting UFO crash case worth mentioning happened in Pennsylvania in 1965. In late afternoon on December 9, 1965, a strange flaming object was seen over Canada, Ohio, and western Pennsylvania. The object crashed just outside of Kecksburg, Pennsylvania, in another controversial UFO crash case.

Numerous witnesses at the site state they saw Army and/or Air Force personnel take something out of the woods early the next morning on a flatbed truck. However, the official explanation was that a meteor was seen streaking through the sky although nothing landed. Several attempts to uncover documents via the Freedom of Information Act (FOIA) has revealed that nothing was collected or discovered in 1965 in Kecksburg by any government agency (Kean). To this day, witnesses still come forward with information to those closest to the case.

Stan Gordon began researching UFO and strange anomalies in western Pennsylvania in 1959 and grew up in Greensburg, Pennsylvania. Greensburg is about 9 miles (as the crow flies) from

Kecksburg. This event fueled his interest in anomalous research to where he still conducts research and investigations to this day in western Pennsylvania and has previously served as a state director for MUFON for the state of Pennsylvania. Stan is convinced that an object did in fact fall from the sky and was procured by government officials that December, but is still on the fence if it was from another planet.

John Ventre, a longtime UFO researcher, former multi-state director for MUFON, and former star of the television show *Hangar 1*, feels that the purported craft is a General Electric Mark-2 reentry vehicle. Ventre was convinced by researcher Owen Eichler of some information that conveniently pointed to many clues that the crash was caused by the reentry vehicle (Ventre 2015a). The vehicle is thought to have been launched by the United States Air Force as a spy satellite, but failed to stay in orbit. Many people feel that this solves the longstanding mystery or at least these latest findings are made to look that way by some (Majors). However, many questions still remain including any verification from any source that a GE Mark-2 vehicle actually landed anywhere in 1965 let alone western Pennsylvania.

I mentioned the Aurora, Texas, crash in the first chapter of this book. It can be added to the above stories and the dozens that have happened since then of purported crashed UFOs. John Ventre documented 39 such cases of crashed craft from 1865 to 1992 (Ventre 2015b). The website for the Center for the Study of Extraterrestrial Intelligence currently lists 272 such accounts of crashed crafts where items or extraterrestrial bodies were recovered (Craddock).

One big connection with UFO crashes, let alone the entire cultural phenomenon, is the purported cover-ups of the story and evidence by the government. Nowhere else in UFO culture is the conspiracy theories more prevalent than with the crash of purported extraterrestrial crafts. Nearly every story that discusses UFO crashes involves some type of purported cover-up by a government agency, whether in the United States or anywhere else in the world. As we have seen, however, many of these crash stories are based on misinterpretation, hoaxes, or even con artists.

The main fuel for conspiracy theories is the cover-up of knowledge and information by those who are able to control it and keeping it from reaching the general public for whatever reason. For us it is easy to blame our lack of evidence on those who control the other aspects of our daily lives. There has been a concentration on freeing up this information from government officials for years especially through the Freedom of Information Act (FOIA) which was created back in 1966. Despite this effort to channel certain pieces of information to the public many still claim that the truth is being hidden and this information is just disinformation.

The conspiracy theory is a complex issue that we will explore in a subsequent chapter that deals with the cultural aspects of belief. Disclosure is typically the chant of those who want the government to release their knowledge on this topic, but many feel that the truth is being hidden. Is it being hidden because we can't handle the truth, they have an agreement of some sort with an alien race, or because of some national security issue? The reality here is that we can't just sit and wait for disclosure of government knowledge of UFOs if we are actually able to get out there and investigate current sightings and related phenomenon for ourselves.

One thing we see with many of these historic UFO crash cases is that the witness statements seem to evolve or blossom over time. On the other side we notice that some witness testimony seems to deteriorate with time. While the average person has a hard time being a witness to many events and details become distorted or forgotten it would surely be amplified over time due to a number of circumstances. When looking at court cases there has been disturbing facts about the inability for people to remember faces and events. Since the 1990s hundreds of wrongly accused prisoners have been exonerated due to DNA testing. In 71% of these instances eyewitness misidentification was the cause (Bohannon). Granted, as already discussed, much of what occurs with UFO witnesses is blatant fabrication as essentially part of their will to believe or at least to participate.

A UFO crash case will more than likely never land on your desk. Obviously the fire department, paramedics, and potentially even the military would respond long before you would get a chance or even

MUFON's Star Team would respond first. The key in this chapter is that prior crash stories have already influenced the culture of UFOs and the difficulty of investigating them is keeping the facts from morphing into a mythology from a variety of witnesses and researchers.

This also underscores the difficult nature of researching and investigating historical cases. When I say historical cases I mean ones that happened more than a few weeks, months, or even years ago where the area or people have changed significantly over time. A historical case in a desert climate would be much older than one, say, in Pennsylvania due to a slower eroding landscape. As already mentioned people's memories also erode just like the landscape, but we'll talk more in-depth about this in a subsequent chapter.

Another key with this chapter is to understand that categorizing cases is essential to understanding how to approach them. A typical UFO sighting is much different than a crash report. For starters, one may report a light in the sky, or seeing an object in both types of cases, but a crash report may not have any witnesses to a craft flying. A crash report generally involves conspiracy theories, cover-ups, and government participation at some level – whether it happened or not. Crash cases are very complex and ones that happened weeks, months, or even years ago may be pretty much impossible to investigate without finding a solid object sticking out of the ground.

From a skeptical, or logical, standpoint we should also consider the rational probability of a craft crash landing on Earth. First, one would have to assume that a craft that has the means of traveling through space, at great speeds, through wormholes, and with obvious advanced technology, would have better chances of surviving a thunderstorm or Earth-based weapons technology (Danelek).

One should also consider that we on Earth did send living people into space, but the first space pioneers were fruit flies, monkeys, and dogs (Dohrer). We are also reaching a point, in our technological infancy, to be able to attempt to build artificially intelligent robots that could fly space craft for extended journeys deep into space. Wouldn't it make sense that a more advanced and intelligent society keep their species intact? What's more, an overwhelming majority of objects shot into space have so far been unmanned and the most distant objects that Earth has put out into space, the furthest launched September 5, 1977, are not coming back.

Chapter 4: Other Aspects of UFOs

Of course, as you may already know, there is a whole lot more to UFOs than just basic sightings and crashes of the craft. From time to time you might receive cases involving other aspects that are typically related to UFO sightings. Again, the relationship to UFOs is generally tied to that of aliens or extraterrestrial biological entities and the other aspects mentioned here typically fit into that category as well.

This chapter is geared toward the discussion of these "fringe" aspects of UFO reports. It is meant to provide an overview of the subject matter leading into the second part of the book where we will look at the cultural and psychological aspects of some of these case types. In the third part we will look at how to document and go about helping a person with these types of cases. This primer chapter will help serve as a layer of understanding of these case types to make it much easier to approach as a researcher and investigator with a level head.

For many, a UFO sighting is a one-time event. They see it when they are driving, taking out the trash, walking the dog, out camping, or doing something else when something extremely interesting gathers their attention for just a few short moments. After that, it's back to normal.

For others, a single sighting turns into another visit, and another, and another. Each visit may bring about a bit more contact from whoever is controlling the craft or sharing information about what their intentions are. Many people claim to be contactees, that is, they are frequently asked by aliens to board crafts or are able to mentally communicate with extraterrestrial biological entities to see alien crafts or to participate in their research. Others, however, don't seem to have much of a choice in the matter.

Antônio Vilas-Boas was ploughing his fields on October 16, 1957, in the state of Minas Gerais in southcentral Brazil. The 23 year old had opted to work at night to avoid the heavy heat of the day. He noticed an odd red light in the sky that continued to seem to get closer and closer to him. He was a bit shocked when he realized it was an egg shaped object with the red light rotating on top of it. As the craft hovered close by attempting to land Antônio attempted to ride away on his tractor, but it had stopped operating leaving him no option but to run.

As he attempted to run he was grabbed by a humanoid and quickly surrounded by others. These humanoids were said to be manlike yet had small blue eyes, wore tight fitting gray uniforms, and communicated with yelps and barks (Birnes). He was dragged aboard a spaceship and stripped of his clothes. After being smeared with a strange gel, having a blood sample drawn, as well as other tests performed another humanoid walked into the room. This humanoid was an odd looking woman who was nude with straight and white hair, catlike eyes, and had red pubic and underarm hair. Antônio stated he felt attracted to her and the two had intercourse. Once completed the female humanoid rubbed her belly and gestured skyward making him feel as though she would have a baby and raise it in space.

Antônio was not happy with this, but was given his clothes back and was eventually dropped off the craft. When he checked the time he realized he had been gone for 4 hours. Despite such an odd story he purportedly stuck with it through the years and had only this one visit from the humanoids. Unfortunately, his story is not believed by many and his story took a bit of time to become public.

João Martins was a Brazilian writer that had been working on a series of stories called "Flying Saucers' Terrible Mission" that appeared in a popular magazine called *O Cruzeiro*. Martins received many letters from readers of their own experiences which Martins had encouraged. One of the letters received Martins' attention and he and the reader exchanged several letters. The letters were sent from Antônio Vilas-Boas who was eventually asked to come to Rio de Janeiro. His story was initially cast aside due to the fact that Antônio admitted his abduction occurred one day after reading an article on similar abduction stories in *O Cruzeiro* (Wolchover).

While his story would be published by a few South American UFO research groups it would eventually get the attention of George Adamski, who would compare these claims to his own and "verify" them because of his experiences. Adamski, meanwhile, had been involved with UFOs since the late 1940s and had become an influential figure in the field especially due to his photographs of UFOs as well as his stories of being a contactee. Nearly all of Adamski's claims that could be verified were found to be fictional and many felt he was nothing more than a con artist.

Many details in the Antônio Vilas-Boas case also pointed to some ridiculous statements and questionable details. Among these were that the alien craft used rope ladders for the humanoids to climb in and out of the craft on. Also, the description of the craft nearly matched that of Sputnik. Even Martins and Dr. Fontes, who examined Antônio when he came to Rio de Janeiro, did not hold much belief in his account.

The Betty and Barney Hill story of abduction is one of the more believable stories on the subject, but even then there are holes and many feel even this popular event may not have happened. September 19, 1961, Betty and Barney Hill were driving home from a vacation to Canada. Barney noticed a strange light in the sky near the moon and the couple stopped a couple of times in order to view it.

At one point they stopped to view the object which was coming closer to them. Barney was able to see the object in detail and could see occupants inside of the flying craft. Panicking, the couple quickly drove off and simultaneously heard a beeping sound. A while later they heard the beeping sound again, but were 35 miles south of where they had initially seen the object. They were able to drive home with no further sightings and slept off the incident.

Betty called her sister the following day who insisted that she report it to the local Air Force base. Betty's sister had seen a UFO years prior and she was sure this would be of interest to the government. Barney was reluctant, but Betty contacted them and gave the details to Pease Air Force Base. Barney wanted to forget the incident, but Betty began to read up on UFOs. About ten days after their sighting Betty began to have nightmares. Her dreams were focused on her and Barney being stopped at a road block and then being taken aboard a flying craft.

The Hills were interviewed by Walter Webb, a scientific advisor for NICAP (National Investigations Committee on Aerial Phenomenon). Weeks later another group of researchers interviewed the Hills and found an interesting question for which the Hills had no answer. Based on their testimony the couple should have been able to return home two hours earlier than when they did. Taking mileage and the timing of their event something was amiss with the information.

Ultimately, the Hills underwent hypnosis to help them with the stress of having dealt with the event. It was then that details emerged that filled in the two hours of missing time. Betty's dreams came to light during these episodes and the couple shared details about what happened that night. Despite this story occurring prior to the popularity of abductees the story has been doubted by numerous researchers and skeptics. Though many others feel this might in fact be the most reliable account ever collected (Hasse).

The Betty and Barney Hill abduction case also featured physical evidence. The dress Betty was wearing the night of the abduction was said to have contained biological matter in the form of an unknown pink powder and had been torn at the lining and zipper. Granted, many feel that this happened due to the age of the garment and that the other aspects could be easily explained. Betty's dress and the files she collected were donated by Kathleen Marden and are now housed at the University of New Hampshire (see UNH in resources for a link to the contents).

These two above cases, Antônio Vilas-Boas and Betty and Barney Hill, showcase the type of event known as an abductee. This is obviously called abductee since these people were taken against their will. These two cases are important to the history of abduction research since they are very early documented cases prior to when the culture has been overflowed with information from books, movies, and television.

The abduction narrative, found in detail in the fourth section of this book in Chapter 1, "Encounter Classifications", will give you a clue as to whether the person feels they were truly abducted. Essentially, the abduction narrative is a typical flow of information of what one experiences during their abduction. Unfortunately, this narrative is found in many books as well as online. Regardless as to whether the person's experience follows this narrative or not these cases should be approached like all others with an open mind that looks both ways before giving in to an explanation.

The abduction narrative simply follows the basic steps of a capture and then examination. Sometimes the person will have dreams or premonitions that the event will take place. After the examination, in some cases, the person abducted will get to talk to the people who abducted them. Typically, messages of peace and good will toward others are told and the aliens state they generally mean no harm despite the events that brought the abductee to the ship. Sometimes the abductee will also get a tour of the ship and will typically pick up information that is eventually passed on to investigators.

After these experiences the abductee typically suddenly finds themselves in the location in which they left or in unfamiliar areas. They tend to forget some of the details at first and many times have lost from a few minutes to a few hours of time since they were last aware of being conscious. With the aftermath the abductee may deal with an array of emotions from fear, shame, paranoia, to feeling singularly important or having an oneness with God.

While abductees might have been forced against their will there are also contactees. As mentioned previously in this chapter, these people are able to choose when they participate with alien tests or are able to ask for a ship to appear. You will probably find more contactees in this day and age, but many contactees will also tell of times when they were taken against their will as well.

Many contactees will have "proof" of their encounters through photographs of blurry lights in the sky, videos of shaky blurry lights in the sky, or harrowing stories that tie in government conspiracies and others who have witnessed their ability to contact a UFO. I may paint a picture of these people being oddities wearing aluminum foil hats, but of the many stories I have seen with the purported evidence I have yet to hear any claims have any substantial proof. Does that mean these events are not happening?

While I would say there could be an underlying psychological issue with many of them there could also be the startling reality that some of them may perceive to have the ability of controlling UFOs or are actually in cahoots with our space brothers. Validation, unfortunately, has yet to have been found in any of these cases. We will explore some of the psychological aspects in the second chapter of Part II.

Something that may explain why abductees are taken and why contactees are able to flag down UFOs may deal with implants. Alien implants have been a part of UFO culture since the late 1950s and picked up in popularity in the 1960s. These implants are thought to either be tracking devices or a form of mind control. Implants tend to be made of ceramic or metal and range in size from a BB to a pinhead.

Dr. Roger Leir, a podiatrist from Thousand Oaks, California, conducted the first real look at alien implants from multiple people who had reported them. He noted that these implants are typically covered in a protein and keratin covering, which some think might just be from surface skin. But, nerves and receptors found near the implants are said to be from the wrong part of the body (Lorgen).

To many who have had implants removed they state they feel "loss" and that a part of themselves were removed with the object.

Others correlate psychic abilities with the implants that are lost when the devices are removed. However, the fact that the membrane surrounding the objects is more than likely surface skin many believe these objects are merely picked up in falls or contact with broken objects (Nickell).

There are other aspects of events that are connected to UFOs, but probably have other explanations. One of the more popular themes connected to UFOs is the subject of cattle mutilations. These are claims that cows, or even horses, dogs, deer, and other animals, are subjected to surgical removal of parts and left for dead on farms or other locations all over the world.

Cattle mutilations actually began with a case of a mutilated horse in Colorado. On September 7, 1967, Lady (though referred to as "Snippy" in most stories) failed to show up for her daily feeding. Nellie Lewis, the owner of the horse, discovered the body of Lady two days later. The skin and flesh had been pulled back from the head and shoulders. Lewis stated numerous details that pointed toward her belief that extraterrestrials were responsible for the death of the horse including laser precision cuts on the skin.

A Denver pathologist claimed that Lady was missing her heart, brain and other organs. A strange odor, odd marks, dead grass, and it was discovered that an area about two city blocks away from Lady's body was radioactive. There was also no blood discovered at the scene and no blood found within the body itself. NICAP (National Investigations Committee on Aerial Phenomena) came to the scene and had documented the local UFO sightings and felt too that this mutilation was somehow related to the sightings.

Dr. Robert Adams, a pathologist with the Condon Commission UFO study performed an autopsy on Lady. His findings were that she had a severe infection in her leg at the time of her death. A slice in the skin near the throat suggests that possibly someone cut her throat to spare the horse's pain. This opening would have led to the brain area being exposed by scavengers and insects. The brain, being mostly fluid, would have evaporated within a couple of weeks. The other organs are typically prime targets of coyotes and other large scavengers. Lady was not extensively examined for at least 30 days after her death.

Dr. Wallace Leary, operator of a local Veterinary Clinic, obtained the corpse of Lady after the autopsies and other work was done with her body in the field. As he boiled the bones to remove the remaining flesh he noticed two small bullet holes in the left pelvis and right thigh bones. He surmised that someone may have shot Lady who then ran into a barbed wire fence from panic (Duran). Of course it's also possible this injury lead to the infection which brought the horse's death.

Cattle mutilations became not only a big focus but a big financial problem in Colorado in the 1970s. The state asked for numerous grants as well as federal help in investigating what was going on. It was estimated that over 8,000 cattle and other farm animals were mutilated in a nine state area with Colorado seemingly receiving the brunt of the damage. The dollar amount was estimated to be at least $1,000,000 (Redfern). The FBI's result was that predators were doing an overwhelming majority of the kills followed by death by sharp instruments and finally by people killing them to seemingly add to the paranoia.

Another interesting observation by many who were dealing with these mutilations was the sighting of many unmarked black or white helicopters that were seen in the area of mutilations. This prompted many to speculate that the government might have had something to do with what was going on. Granted, by officially putting the blame on predators, scavengers, random accidents, and perhaps insurance fraud, the government conveniently sidestepped any possibility of having to pay any money for the damages.

Is there a UFO connection? Many say yes, due to laser precision cuts, no blood, and the fact that many animals seemed to have just dropped from the sky. The first few explanations fit with an animal that has been dead a while before being closely inspected. The last detail might also pin the blame on the secret helicopters. While there were many UFO sightings in the areas where mutilations were high this does not justify drawing a straight line between the two.

One last thing to explore that is many times said to be caused from UFO sightings are crop circles. It would probably be pretty rare for you to get a crop circle case, unless you are from England but they do happen from time to time in many U.S. states and Canadian provinces. Crop circles are essentially a pattern of downed crop in a field that displays a geometric pattern or merely a large circle.

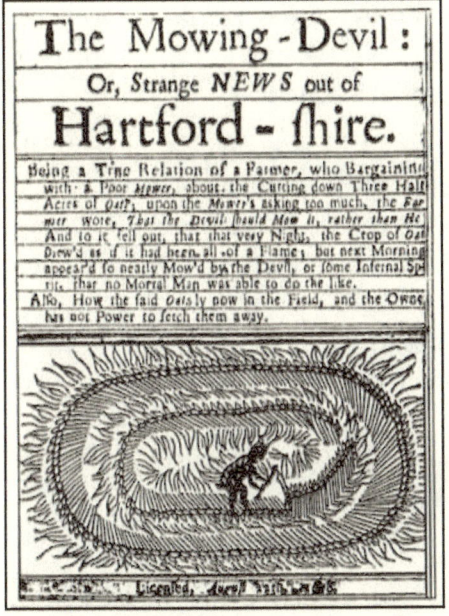

The Mowing-Devil:
Or, Strange NEWS out of
Hartford - fhire.

Being a True Relation of a Farmer, who Bargaining with a Poor Mower, about the Cutting down Three Half Acres of Oats, upon the Mower's asking too much, the Farmer swore, That the Devil should Mow it, rather than He. And so it fell out, that that very Night, the Crop of Oat shew'd as if it had been all of a Flame, but next Morning appear'd so neatly Mow'd by the Devil, or some Infernal Spirit, that no Mortal Man was able to do the like. Also, How the said Oats ly now in the Field, and the Owner has not Power to fetch them away.

Licensed, Aug 22 1678

Many who research crop circles or UFOs have heard of the woodcut of the "Mowing Devil". To many, this justifies modern day UFOs since "they've been happening since 1678" more or less validates today's complex patterns. Actually, no, it doesn't.

The "Mowing-Devil: or, Strange News out of Hartford-shire", is a woodcut pamphlet that was indeed published in 1678. The issue is the story says that the farmer in Hertfordshire refused to pay the sum to have his lawn mowed. He stated that he'd rather have the devil do it instead of paying such a high price. The next morning the lawn was perfectly mowed. The cutout reads:

"Being a True Relation of a Farmer, who Bargaining with a poor Mower, about the Cutting down Three Half Acres of Oats upon the Mower's asking too much, the Farmer swore, 'That the Devil should Mow it, rather than He.' And lo it fell out, that that very Night, the Crop of Oats shew'd as if it had been all of a Flame, but next Morning appear'd so neatly Mow'd by the Devil, or some Infernal Spirit, that no Mortal Man was able to do the like. Also, How the said Oats ly now in the Field, and the Owner has not Power to fetch them away." (Mowing-devil).

One big observation here is that the lawn was cut, not laid down like modern crop circles. It seems that the imagery of a devil cutting the grass in the pattern observed on the woodcut is what makes people think this has to do with crop circles.

Modern day crop circle reports are said to be traced back to 1937. There are a few descriptions of what sounds like crop circles coming from the 1950s and 1960s, but it was the 1980s when the world went crop circle crazy. The term "crop circle" is attributed to Colin Andrews who first mentioned it in his first book, *Circular Evidence*, in 1989. The first person to investigate and report crop circles, a colleague of Andrews, was Pat Delgado (Talbott).

Delgado and Andrews were the first of many cereologists, those who study crop circles, and the popularity and interest in the phenomenon continued to grow in the early 1990s. In 1991, Doug Bower and David Chorley invited Delgado to inspect a crop circle that they had discovered. Delgado walked through it with journalists and other members of the media in tow. He was very certain that this was a genuine crop circle and was convinced it had not been faked.

However, it was quickly revealed that Bower and Chorley, popularly known as Doug and Dave, had created the circle right in front of the journalists. Doug and Dave claimed that they were responsible for a majority of crop circles prior to 1987 and over 200 of them from 1987 to 1991. One would think this would be the end of the line for crop circles as it was for Delgado who quit the field shortly after the incident (Andrews). However, after this announcement and the worldwide attention to crop circles, there became a boom in circle formations that continued well into the 1990s.

Bower had visited Australia where he saw media reports of an impression in swampland that accompanied a UFO sighting. Once back in England he convinced his friend Chorley to create fake circles on a Friday pub night (Smallwood). They had no attention until a 1981 circle at Cheesefoot head that could be seen by people was created. The crop circle gained instant international attention and as they continued to fabricate circles an entire industry of investigators and experts, books, and other types of media was created around the belief driven by the fake circles. Once the pair heard word that the government was going to create an inquiry about the circles they decided they had enough fun and came clean (Geraghty). The pair had been creating the circles since 1976 just for the fun of it, but the craze had gotten a little out of hand.

While neither man seemed to profit from these creations, with the exception of a few thousand dollars of their exclusive story of their reveal to *Today Newspaper*, it was claimed at the time that they were part of a conspiracy. The conspiracy involved Mi5, also known as the Security Service and is the United Kingdom's domestic counter-intelligence and security agency, although the pair dismissed the idea with a laugh. Even if they were commissioned by the government their creation of fake circles helped generate a worldwide interest and the current culture of belief that exists today – so if it was a plan to discredit - the plan surely backfired.

Crop circles continue to form all over the world to this day. Many researchers have taken an interest into their formation, but the focus is not on UFOs but it is believed that most are created by people. One interesting aspect is that crop circles have become more complex than what they have ever appeared in the past. Part of this is geared toward new technology including global positioning satellites, lasers, computers, and possibly even portable machines that create microwaves to carefully bend stalk instead of the plank and rope systems of Doug and Dave's days (Taylor).

Part II: I Want to Believe

Chapter 1: The Culture of UFO Belief

Sunday, October 30, 1938, 8 PM, the Columbia Broadcasting System radio network in New York City began presenting their 17th episode of *The Mercury Theatre on the Air* live radio drama. That week's episode was titled, *The War of the Worlds* and would become one of the most well-known radio moments and most interesting pieces of UFO culture in history. The radio program broadcasted what appeared to be live radio coverage of a purported invasion of UFOs and Martians over Grover's Mill, New Jersey. The show began with a warning that it was just a dramatization, but many tuned in to the middle of the program which caused a bit of confusion and concern.

The show, while complete fiction, was believed by many to be real coverage of a Martian invasion. Police even came to the studio in an attempt to shut the show down (Vallance). While the reaction to the radio program is largely exaggerated over time there was still a lot of public backlash toward the radio station as well as toward Orson Welles who produced the show due to the confusion it created. This public attention led to very productive career for Welles in Hollywood which lasted until his death in 1985.

On February 12, 1949, Radio Quito in Quito, Ecuador, did their own live version of *The War of the Worlds* using the basic storyline from Welles. Unfortunately, they took their stunt a little too far and many of those listening truly thought an invasion was under way. When the radio station realized this they immediately stated that the show was a dramatization and that everyone was safe. This plan backfired; many people had confessed their sins in public and panic had spread to the streets. An angry mob headed to the radio station which was housed in a larger building and set fire to it injuring dozens and killing 6 people (Alvear).

This fear reaction to *The War of the Worlds* broadcasts has been used as a basis for one of the most longstanding conspiracy theories about UFOs and the government. Many believe, just based off of this radio show, that the government feels the general public cannot handle the truth of UFOs and aliens. This broadcast alone is purportedly an underscore of the evidence gathered that the public should not be told about what is known about UFOs and extraterrestrials. Unfortunately, newspapers are largely to blame for creating a bit larger of a story than what actually happened during the original broadcast and there was not much of a panic in New York City (Pooley, Socolow). While it might have been possible to cover up crashed craft in the 1940s I would think it would be virtually impossible in the 21st century with cell phones, social media, and 24 hour television news.

Part of the fear involving *The War of the Worlds* was that the United States was facing a real war threat at the time. Some people during the 1938 broadcast initially thought that the Germans were attacking the United States. During the Quito broadcast many locals thought that neighboring Peru had been attacking Ecuador (Gosling). Still, the threat of UFOs attacking was not taken lightly by many listening in. While many listening to both broadcasts were keenly aware it was a dramatization through the initial announcement preceding the show others were obviously in pure belief that this event was truly happening.

A similar radio drama surrounding a mock alien takeover occurred on August 27, 2013, at a radio station in Tuscumbia, Alabama. The station merely broadcasted a series of conversations between a man (known as the "Commander") and woman, purportedly aliens, that were evaluating humanity and the radio signal that lead them to Earth. The purported alien "takeover" and hacking of the station was used to announce a format change for Star 94.9 FM for the following day.

The broadcast was an obvious radio drama from the content used including talking about the station's Facebook page, Twerking, reading the book *Goodnight Moon*, and discussing an addiction to playing the game Candy Crush. However, many people were panicking and called the radio station as well as the police (Scherker). Some were so upset from the broadcast that some children were afraid to go to school the following morning after the gag started.

Parents had panicked thinking there was a bomb threat that was thought to have come from the messages, but this was mere speculation from rumors that snowballed. The regional director of programming for Schols Radio group, Brian Rickman, stated that he had no idea that this would lead to any concerns, but he and many others were amazed at this reaction.

We should also remember that H.G. Wells published the book *The War of the Worlds* in 1897. While it was not a huge seller it still had an impact on UFO and alien culture. Books have had a large impact on various aspects of UFO culture from abductions to the aforementioned alien attacks. Many of these books lead to movie adaptations such as the 1955 novel *The Body Snatchers*. This book was the obvious source to the movie *Invasion of the Body Snatchers* in 1956 which was then remade in 1978, 1993, and another adaptation in 2007.

The War of the Worlds was also created into a movie in 1953. It has since been remade in 2005 by Steven Spielberg and spawned a few other movies as well. The movie *Invaders from Mars* was pushed into release in 1953 just ahead of *The War of the Worlds*. This movie is known to have put aliens and their flying saucers in color on screen for the first time. There were plenty of alien based movies to follow in the 1950s and 1960s most of which were based on alien invasions.

Comic books began in 1825, but the "golden age" was the 1930s where numerous characters entertained children and adults alike. One of the many factions of comic books is that of superheroes (Kraska). Superheroes were looked up to by children and still are today. Nearly all of these characters have some sort of super ability that makes them stronger or smarter than your average person, some have supernatural or paranormal abilities, others have been able live prolonged periods of time, and others are based on aliens.

Comics have always been viewed by adults as a disposable form of entertainment that may play a small role in development but is otherwise meaningless. In the latter part of the 20th century many scholars researched the importance of comic books in the social development of children and comic books were finally "valued" as something of importance (Johnson). If children look up to these comic books and learn social development from them wouldn't you think the themes of aliens and alien invasions would have a potential long term affect as well?

Superman is considered to be one of the top superhero comic book characters and one of the first. Sure you had other costumed heroes and ones who fought aliens such as Buck Rogers, Flash Gordon, Green Hornet, John Carter, the Phantom, and others, but Superman was the first hero from another planet. Superman is an interesting character since, according to his original origin in *Action Comics* #1, he is dispelled from his planet as a baby due to it crumbling from old age. He displays super strength, speed, and durability that are justified when looking at how strong an ant is and how high a grasshopper can jump at scale to humans. Superman's initial purpose was to help the oppressed and was essentially a vigilante due to the Great Depression era that welcomed such a hero. This was a new look at aliens altogether as for the first time an alien was popular with the public and this one was benefitting mankind.

Of course Superman's origin story and purpose in life has changed with the times. He is still considered one of the most popular characters and has produced numerous movies, television shows, and still appears in comic books. Obviously characters like Superman have helped spawn other alien heroes and villains which have helped create the other media that entertain the masses.

The television show *Star Trek*, which aired from 1966 to 1969, spawned five other television series and 13 movies to date and has become a fixture of alien culture. Interestingly, the basic concept of the show is that humans are the ones exploring space and are essentially the alien invaders. Granted, many of the aliens encountered are up to no good and leave the viewer with the thought that most alien races are essentially greedy or otherwise evil despite our best intentions of bringing peace to the galaxy.

This famous series was actually preceded by the *Lost in Space* television show that ran from 1965 to 1968. *Lost in Space* and *Star Trek* were both cancelled after three seasons due to poor ratings and *Lost in Space* had more episodes 83 to 79, but syndication made *Star Trek* one of the most prominent franchises in movie and television history.

It is startling to think about how many movies are made in modern times which deal with aliens to varying degrees. Those early movies may look cheesy to us now, but they helped shape how we perceived aliens and how Hollywood would continue to use them in movies.

The number one grossing movie of 1968 was *2001: A Space Odyssey*. This movie explored many concepts of aliens including their influence on the human race. A sequel released in 1984, named *2010*, focused on the realization that an intelligent life form exists.

The 1970s brought the beginning of the *Star Wars* franchise. The 1977 movie was actually the fourth episode in the space opera saga yet the first one to kick off the series. Sequels were released in 1980, 1983, 2015, and 2017, while prequels were released 1999, 2002, and 2005. The original movie has inspired cartoons, comic books, numerous books cataloging thousands of years of pseudohistory, a never ending line of toys, and even a religion based on the Jedi. This franchise is set "in a galaxy far, far away" and doesn't necessarily seem to affect us here on Earth. But, this whole galaxy of characters, planets, and space politics has created what I feel is a sort of comfort zone toward potential alien visitors although most certainly overshadowed by other movies on hostile takeover themes.

Also in 1977 was the movie *Close Encounters of the Third Kind*. This movie explores many facets of UFOs and aliens including visitations earlier in history, abductions, contactees, government cover-ups, and initial contact with the human race. In 1979 there was *Alien*. This movie does not present a pleasant thought about contact with alien creatures as it is meant to be a science fiction horror film and treats aliens as viruses. This popular franchise has also created three sequels, two crossover films with the *Predator* franchise, and two prequels *Prometheus* and *Alien: Covenant*.

The 1980s brought some feel-good alien movies with *E.T. the Extra-terrestrial* in 1982, *The Last Starfighter* in 1984, and the animated *Transformers: The Movie* in 1986. *E.T. the Extraterrestrial* portrayed the loveable alien as a botanist turned displaced alien (due to pesky government agents) who fought for its life in the attempt to be rescued and return home. This is a welcomed concept from Steven Spielberg who is responsible for many alien based movies.

The Last Starfighter is probably one that many don't remember or have not seen. This one, I feel, is important since it portrays an alien race recruiting a human through a video game to help them fight a competing alien race. This movie gives us a glimmer of hope that maybe aliens might need us for something more than energy, a planet, or as food.

The Transformers cartoon series enthralled children from 1986 to 1987 and even spawned a cartoon movie in 1986. The premise of this is that an advanced alien race of robots crash landed on Earth millions of years ago. The two factions of good and evil (Autobots and Decepticons) are here to help Earth and humans as well as constantly fight over Earth's resources respectively. The franchise has gone on to produce even more animated series as well as live action movies that are still being announced in the future.

One spellbinding television show of the mid-1980s was *V*. *V* was initially a miniseries with two episodes that ran for a total of 189 minutes in early 1983. The following year *V: The Final Battle* ran with three episodes with a total of 272 minutes and from late 1984 to early 1985 a 19 episode season of *V* aired. The premise of the show is that an alien race comes to Earth for aid for their planet, yet turns out to be a race of carnivorous reptilian humanoids with a sweet tooth for humans that have manipulated the world's governments and are set on taking over Earth. A remake of *V* aired from 2009 to 2011 with 2 seasons and a total of 22 episodes.

The 1990s and the UFO and alien concepts in movies and television was highlighted by *The X Files*. This series which started in 1993 lasted until 2002 with nine seasons only to return for season ten in 2016 and an announced return for season 11. During its run it also had two movies, two spinoff television series, as well as books and comic books devoted to it. While the premise of the series is about the paranormal in general the core of the series dealt with an ongoing government conspiracy involving aliens in various scenarios and tackled many concepts including abductions, implants, contactees, alien invasions, and many other notions that solidified UFOs and aliens in popular culture.

Since then things have not let up in Hollywood in regards to aliens. *Stargate* (1994) focuses on aliens having an influence on the past similar to ancient alien theories. The movie would launch a franchise which included three television series, two movies, books as well as comic books and a video game. *Species* (1995) centers on receiving communications from an alien race that lead to the creation of an alien-human hybrid. This movie would also inspire further movies as well as a book and a comic book series. Species is also noted to be the root of modern Chupacabra sightings that occurred in Puerto Rico just after the release of the movie in July of 1995. The first actual witness of the Chupacabra, Madelyne Tolentino, described the creature as looking nearly exact to the character of Sil from the movie (Radford, 2011a).

In 1997 there was the movie *Starship Troopers*. The movie is based on a book and focuses on Earth battling aliens that are giant warring insects. The movie *Men in Black* (1997) is more or less an action comedy features the secret organization which essentially monitors extraterrestrials and attempts to keep them a secret from regular society. This franchise inspired two more movies and a cartoon and is rumored to be ready for a reboot. In between all of these movies are other ones that inspire a bit of fear. *Predator* (1987) and sequels *Predator 2* (1990), *Predators* (2010), as well as the previously mentioned two crossover movies with the *Alien* movie franchise, featured aliens that hunted humans for sport. *They Live* (1988), *Independence Day* (1996) and the sequel, *Independence Day: Resurgence* (2016) all feature alien invasions. *Signs* (2002) used crop circles as a catalyst for an alien invasion movie. *The Fourth Kind* (2009) focuses on alien abductions and is geared toward making the viewer think these are actual cases.

Just looking at movies released in 2016 we see *Rogue One: A Star Wars Story, Captain America: Civil War, Star Trek Beyond, Arrival, Batman v Superman: Dawn of Justice, The Great Wall, Independence Day: Resurgence, Passengers, Max Steel, Warcraft: The Beginning, The 5ᵗʰ Wave, 10 Cloverfield Lane,* and many other lesser known movies all featuring aliens to one degree or another and just as many in 2017. As of June, 2017, four of the top ten and nine of the top twenty highest grossing movies (not adjusted for inflation) of all time involve aliens (The Numbers). Sadly, a majority of these movies portray aliens as evil or with bad intentions of some sort especially toward humans.

This isn't meant to be an inclusive list of movies, television shows and other forms of media dealing with aliens and UFOs as I'm sure there are a few that you have thought of that I failed to mention. This chapter merely serves as a reminder to the reader that there are an overwhelming amount of cultural references to UFOs, aliens, abductions, and many other aspects to this field that affect everyday people in how they view the subject. While there are quite a few horror movies that deal with ghosts there are far greater entertainment based cultural references to aliens and UFOs than ghosts and cryptids combined.

As we have seen most movies portray aliens as having evil

intentions. We might consider alien themed movies to be just another form of entertainment, but as we see the mounting number of movies we should feel how heavy they weigh on how public opinion is formed on the topic.

Books, movies, and other media affect us not just general fear of aliens due to their conditioning of invasions but also with specific areas of the phenomenon. The theoretical physicist and cosmologist Stephen Hawking even created a bit of fear in 2010 when he stated that alien contact was just inviting bad things. His thought was that inviting aliens was akin to Christopher Columbus discovering the Americas and the subsequent colonization of many areas through hostile takeovers and bloody battles (Hickman). Granted, these statements were more than likely made to hype his new television show *Into the Universe with Stephen Hawking*, which was one of many he was involved in. But all of this has taken a toll on our perception of aliens and of UFOs.

The psychology of belief is a very powerful thing. The unknown generally sparks fear in most people since it goes beyond our everyday understanding of the world. In regards to aliens and UFOs the fear comes from not understanding what is about to happen or basing the potential on what we have learned through other pieces of culture including books and movies. Dealing with perceived UFOs or alien contact can be created from a number of physiological perceptions and psychological reactions as we will now explore.

Chapter 2: The Truth is Out There

March 13, 1997, Phoenix, Arizona, numerous witnesses claimed to see a large triangular shaped UFO in the sky heading north to south across the state. In Phoenix, bright lights hanging in the sky were filmed by numerous witnesses. The lights, as we have already mentioned, are likely nothing more than military flares dropped during a training exercise. While this incident and the details surrounding another craft with this particular sighting are still debated a subsequent mass UFO event over Phoenix in April of 2008 was quickly solved.

On April 21, 2008, hundreds of witnesses frantically called police and the media to report four bright red lights that seemed to form a triangular UFO that slowly morphed in shape (Radford 2008). The event had some people worried that the UFOs from 1997 had returned. In fact, in 2007 UFOs were also reported, but these turned out to be flares dropped from an F-16 which was quickly solved. The 2008 incident seemed like a repeat of 1997 as residents and the media initially seemed baffled as to what the lights might have been. Luke Air Force Base was quick to admit that they definitely did not have anything in the sky during this sighting so flares would not be an explanation this time around.

This media focus once again on the lights over Phoenix actually helped solved the mystery. The following afternoon Lino Mailo contacted *The Arizona Republic* newspaper. Mailo stated that he had witnessed his neighbor release helium balloons with flares attached to them around 8 PM that night (Fowle). He didn't realize the media buzz that would have accompanied this seemingly innocent action or he said he would have filmed the man in the act for verification of his claim.

The following day the neighbor did come forward anonymously and admitted he had tied the flares to fishing line and let them go in 15 minute increments (McGaha and Nickell). Another "Phoenix Lights" mystery was solved and many began to think that this latest prank made the previous events less believable as well. What began as mild panic about a potential alien invasion was now viewed as a complex series of pranks even though these were all separate incidents.

Could simple flares create panic of a UFO over a major city? Well, it wasn't quite panic in Phoenix, but many other sightings all over the world of flares, airplanes, and other misidentified objects in the sky have created mild confusion or panic locally as well as through social media. I have personally documented no less than a dozen stories that I can recall for my radio broadcast, the *Paranormal News Insider*, since 2008 that dealt with flares, aircraft, or other simple explanations for lights in the sky all over the world. These explanations might be simple after the fact, but during the time the witness was seeing it their perspective was that this was definitely an unidentified flying object and not in the context of not being able to identifying but in the context of, well, aliens.

As we have already read there are many cultural references of UFOs and aliens that make the idea of witnessing one not completely implausible. Granted, no one gets up and think they will see one that afternoon but the seed has been planted for us by these prior references and all our minds need is a little water to get the plant of belief growing. Once our mind is fooled into thinking we've seen something completely out of the ordinary it takes the mind a little time to "come back to Earth", that is, if we allow it.

We have already discussed some of the beliefs behind UFOs and aliens such as crop circles, cattle mutilations, abductions, and so on. We have already addressed where some of these beliefs might have come from such as movies, comic books, books, as well as the beliefs of others. I have already shot down most of the evidence about many of the famous sightings, crashes, stories, and even beliefs behind UFOs and aliens. However, I do not mean to discourage the believer or those who desire to validate these claims. My goal with this book is to provide a balance of belief by presenting the evidence of both sides.

It is hard to maintain a balance with anything in life let alone anomalous or paranormal research. We all have biases and we all have our beliefs. I have attempted to keep this book balanced but to you it may seem a bit skeptical. While you may have strong beliefs regarding UFOs and related phenomenon you may find yourself judging someone else who has beliefs that seem "kooky" or way too far "out there" to be believable. It's all about perspective. While researching the psychology of belief (which is one of my favorite topics) I ran across this quote which fits perfectly into this book. This quote comes from Alex Lickerman, M.D. and an article he wrote titled, *The Two Kinds of Belief: Why infants reason better than adults*. This quote fits how others may view both those who believe and those who do not believe in UFOs and related phenomenon.

"But if we look down upon people who seem blind to evidence that we ourselves find compelling, imagining ourselves to be paragons of reason and immune to believing erroneous conclusions as a result of the influence of our own pre-existing beliefs, more likely than not we're only deceiving ourselves about the strength of our objectivity. Certainly, some of us are better at managing our biases than others, but all of us have biases with which we must contend."

A skeptic might seem a bit close minded to the possibilities that exist in regards to UFOs being reported all over the Earth. With so many witnesses how can believers be wrong? On the other hand, skeptics will say, "Where is the evidence?" Beyond personal experiences with scant evidence that provides no overwhelming data it might appear that believers might be closed minded to common sense and reasoning or the lack of true evidence in the phenomenon they defend.

So, no matter which side you take this quote should help you understand that just because you believe something doesn't make it true. We should stop looking at beliefs, especially in fringe topics such as UFOs, in terms of believers and skeptics. Just like most things in life the truth is typically somewhere in the middle, maybe not the exact center but certainly not at one extreme or the other.

Our personal perspectives can get in the way of viewing a case or a person for that matter. I can't stress enough that as researchers and investigators we must be aware of our personal beliefs and biases and do our best to keep them out of judgement of people and situations. It is critical that we allow evidence and findings dictate the direction or believability of a case over emotions. It's not possible to overcome many of our preconceived emotional responses based on belief, but as long as we are aware of what we believe and that there are counteracting beliefs existing we have a chance to keep emotional reactions to a minimum.

I guess the major point here is really that in investigating fantastic claims we should really understand where we stand on these issues before becoming involved in dealing with people with these dynamic issues. Becoming objective (or non-judgmental) in these types of cases is pretty much impossible and while the focus should be on the evidence alone we will have to take the witness testimony into consideration no matter how fantastic the story may seem. We might not understand them and at times we might not believe them.

A poll conducted in September of 2015 by YouGov found that

56% of Germans, 54% of Americans, and 52% of people in Britain believe that there is extraterrestrial intelligent life. This same poll also found that men were more likely to believe in intelligent aliens than women (Dahlgreen).

A 2012 survey of 1,114 people over the age of 18 by National Geographic revealed that 36% of Americans believed that UFOs exist. This survey also revealed that 77% of Americans believe that aliens have visited the Earth in the past. Granted, this was not a formal scientific poll as it was created in anticipation of a television show *Chasing UFOs* that was soon to be released (and didn't do so well). The survey also asked the question, "Who would you enlist to battle an alien invasion: the Hulk, Batman or Spider-Man?" For this question, 21% responded the Hulk, 12% would call Batman, and only 8% would reach out to Spiderman (DiBlasio).

One of the first polls about UFO perception was conducted by the Gallup Poll organization on August 15, 1947, just less than two months after the Kenneth Arnold sighting and a month after the purported Roswell incident. This poll indicated that roughly 90% of the United States population knew what a UFO was (actually phrased "flying saucer") by hearing or reading about them. However, 39% responded that UFOs more than likely had a logical explanation and less than 1% of those polled thought that UFOs offered any type of threat or problem for the country (Miller).

One important finding within the multitude of polls that look at belief in UFOs to belief in conspiracy theories, ghosts, Bigfoot, and other strange things, is that education does not seem to be any type of indicator of belief despite the claims of some. Polls can show how many people believe in what as well as the background of those who believe but it cannot with certainty explain just why someone believes in such things. There are many books on this topic and it's not this book's goal to define why people believe as we are focused on how to solve the mystery behind the sighting.

It is important, however, for this book to discuss what might lead to such beliefs. For some a single sighting might be all they ever have in their lifetime, but this single sighting can have a powerful effect on how they perceive the subject of UFOs or even ghosts or cryptozoology for that matter. Just as someone might see a bear and think they saw a Bigfoot someone might see an airplane, Chinese or sky lantern, or something else explainable and with these cultural references behind them might jump to the conclusion that they saw something unexplainable.

The American public grew a bit weary of what UFOs might be, but it was the Air Force that began to look into reports to see if there might be a legitimate cause for concern for national security. The Central Intelligence Agency (CIA) began to focus on compiling information on UFOs not because of the potential for conflict with extraterrestrial beings, but because the concern was that this might be Soviet technology with the emergence of the Cold War in 1947 (Haines).

The United States government began investigating UFOs with Project Sign in 1948. They did realize that UFOs were in fact real, but they were neither Soviet technology nor were they alien spacecraft. Most UFOs came down to one of three explanations; mass hysteria and hallucination, hoax, or misinterpretation of known objects (Haines).

Project Grudge followed Sign in 1949 with more of a focus on educating the general public on their findings, but this began to backfire as many felt the government was covering up what they knew. Project Blue Book began in 1952 and lasted until the end of 1969 collecting 12,618 reports with 701 remaining as "unidentified". They felt that these remaining "unidentified" cases were not extraterrestrial vehicles and none of the cases were beyond the range of scientific knowledge or a threat to national security and thus all inquiry into the phenomenon were terminated (Project Blue Book).

A minority of people began to feel that the government was burying what they knew about UFOs when they pulled the plug on these projects. The *Condon Report*, formally titled *Scientific Study of Unidentified Flying Objects*, was published in 1968 and contained data collected by the University of Colorado UFO Project group (known as the Condon Committee) and was a way that a civilian panel could interpret the UFO information. Lead by physicist

Edward Condon the report concluded after two years (November 1966 to November 1968) that the UFO issue was of little value to the scientific community.

Many involved in newly formed civilian UFO research and investigation groups (NICAP, 1956, APRO, 1952) questioned these results and felt that there was a cover-up. However, membership in these civilian organizations began to decline sharply immediately after the Condon Report was published. UFO reports took a sharp decline until the early 1970s although the public viewed them a bit differently after seeing Earthlings walking on the moon on television.

Looking ahead to the third part of this book we can now begin to look at some logical explanations for UFOs. When investigating reports of UFOs the focus should be on finding the answer to what the witness saw, but a search for potential explanations should always be conducted prior to accepting an alien explanation. A serious search for a logical explanation should always take precedence since the answer will generally lay in one of these following examples.

Airplanes get quite a chunk of blame for UFOs, but they are easy to track and identify if you know what you are looking for. The simplest thing to remember about airplanes is that they have strobe lights on them and one wing has a red strobe and the other has a green strobe. The saying, "red right return" is a simple way to remember which wing has what color light. If the plane is coming at you the red light will be on the right. That is essentially saying that the left wing will have a red strobe and the right wing will have a green strobe. This isn't for pedestrians or even air traffic control, but for visualization of aircraft. The series of red and green lights are also used for nautical travel as well and are called navigation lights. However, they are not used for navigation but for positioning as it allows other craft to determine if other craft are approaching or what direction they are flying.

Aircraft are many times thought to be UFOs when they are miles away and heading toward the viewer. Aircraft may actually turn various lights on and off depending upon elevation and conditions.

Landing lights might be on if the plane is under 10,000 feet or flying through a busy air corridor or if the particular airline has a policy for it to be on all the time or at other elevations. Some commercial jets will run with their landing lights on during the day or only at night. These lights are very bright and even in daylight it is possible to see them as much as 50 or more miles away.

Seeing these lights at such distances can create some interesting perceptions. At this distance the light may look stationary and will generally be off white or even yellowish due to the atmospheric conditions. As a plane banks the light will slowly go out and if a jet is making adjustments in flight it might appear that the lights are going on and off. At such great distances the strobe lights will not be visible and sometimes pilots will even turn these strobe lights off which can further confuse someone on the ground who isn't sure what they are seeing.

Stars, **planets**, **meteors**, and even **satellites** are another set of explanations for UFOs that are frequently misidentified. Meteors should be a pretty obvious reason for misinterpretation. A bright meteor

Annual Meteor Shower Calendar

Meteor Shower	Approx Peak Date	Constellation to look towards	Avg Zenith per hour	Originates From
Quadrantids	4-Jan	Bootes	120	not known
Alpha Centaurids	8-Feb	Centaurus	6	not known
Lyrids	22-Apr	Lyra	20	Comet Thatcher
Pi-Puppids	23-Apr	Puppis	variable	not known
Eta-Aquarid	5-May	Aquarius	60	Halley's Comet
June Bootids	27-Jun	Bootes	variable	not known
South Delta-Aquarids	28-Jul	Aquarius	20	not known
Perseids	12-Aug	Perseus	90	Comet Swift-Tuttle
Aurigids	1-Sep	Auriga	variable	not known
Draconids	8-Oct	Draco	variable	not known
Orionids	21-Oct	Orion	20	Halley's Comet
S. Taurid	5-Nov	Taurus	10	not known
N. Taurid	12-Nov	Taurus	15	not known
Leonids	17-Nov	Leo	15	Comet Temple-Tuttle
Alpha-Monocerotids	21-Nov	Monoceros	variable	not known
Dec Phoenicids	6-Dec	Phoenix	variable	not known
Puppid/Velids	6-Dec	Puppis	10	not known
Geminids	13-Dec	Gemini	120	Asteroid 3200 Phaethon
Ursid	22-Dec	Ursa Minor	10	not known

streaking through the sky can appear to be red, orange, or even green or white depending upon what it is made of. Bright flashes can be seen for many miles and may or may not accompany sonic booms. Some large meteorites might be large enough to create such a bright streak from colliding with the atmosphere that it can turn night into day and can also create sonic booms that can shatter windows. One of the largest meteor events in recent times was the Chelyabinsk meteor in Russia that broke up on February 15, 2013, and was estimated to be 65 feet across when it began to fall to Earth. The subsequent shock wave from its entry broke windows from over 7,000 buildings which was the major reason behind the more than 1,500 injuries although no one was reportedly killed (*see* http://www.amsmeteors.org/ *for an up to date meteor shower listing by year*).

Satellites are not frequently seen by most people, but many people who walk their dogs at night or anyone who stares at the night sky might see these strange lights moving above. A satellite may sometimes catch the setting sun just right and cause a flash in the sky that will last longer than a meteor. These reflections are known as satellite flares, glints, or iridium flares. This reflection of light can happen even when the sun has set due to the elevation of the satellite. There are over 35,000 satellites around the Earth ranging from softball sizes of debris to objects larger than 20 feet across. Of these 35,000 objects most are just space junk, or debris, that serve no purpose and of all of these only a handful are visible to the naked eye (Rao).

The largest manmade object in the sky is the International Space Station. This can easily be seen in the night sky and is most visible when reflecting sunlight off of it while flying by after twilight. The ISS has large solar panels that might reflect straight down to the viewer creating flares and along with its tremendous speed it is a highly visible object overhead which can confuse observers who don't know what it is they are seeing (see http://www.space.com/32054-satellite-tracker.html for live tracking of the ISS, the Hubble telescope, and other large satellites and http://www.stellarium.org/ for historical information on star and satellite positions).

The brightest satellites will be seen within an hour of sunset due to the sky being dark yet the satellite being able to reflect sunlight to the observer on the ground. The higher the angle from the observer will also produce a brighter reflection and will be easier to see due to less disruption from light pollution. The satellite may also seemingly disappear as one is viewing it due to slipping into the Earth's shadow and it will no longer reflect sunlight to the observer, this will typically happen if you are observing satellites more than an hour after sunset.

On July 14, 2017, a Soyuz rocket will launch from Kazakhstan that is rumored to be the brightest object in the sky behind the sun and moon. It might end up being a little less bright than Venus, but this crowdsourced cubesat project named Mayak ("lighthouse" in Russian) created by a group of young scientists named "Your sector of space" and supported by Moscow State University of Mechanical Engineering aims to be the brightest manmade object in space and will perform other basic tests. This small satellite will unfurl into a 170 square foot four sided triangle that will reflect 95% of light as it spins once per second overhead (Seaburn). This privately launched satellite will certainly be a cause for many UFO sightings and will be the focus in mid-2017 until the total solar eclipse over the United States on August 21, 2017.

Stars will slowly begin shine at dusk and will sometimes seem to "suddenly" appear and be brighter that what they seem like they should be. Stars and planets will also appear to "move" as the night goes on due to the rotation of the Earth. Since planets are far closer to Earth than any star they will appear to move "quicker" than any star in the sky. The brightness and apparent movement over time is probably why they are attributed to UFO sightings. Mercury, Venus, Mars, Jupiter, and Saturn (and of course Earth) are all visible to the naked eye without a telescope with Venus typically being the brightest and the one to most often be confused with a UFO.

Another aspect of stars and planets that fool us is the fact that they seem to blink. Scintillation is the term to describe twinkling stars in the sky. Stars seem to twinkle because they are a great distance from Earth and their light is but a mere fraction of what it is from close up (think about the sun which is an average sized star). At such a distance that light has to go through our atmosphere here on Earth which consists of varying temperature differences which staggers this light as it approaches our eyes. The staggering of light through the atmosphere leads to the apparent twinkling of stars. Planets will also scintillate, but it will be far less than what a star will since the light (sunlight reflecting off of them) travels a far less distance (Byrd).

Other physical objects might also be confused for UFOs include **dirigibles** (airships), **clouds, weather balloons,** and **regular balloons, Chinese lanterns,** flocks of **birds, kites, parachutes,** and **drones.** The most popular dirigible is the Goodyear Blimp. I am fortunate to have grown up in northeast Ohio and am very familiar with seeing the old gray blimp and now the blue and yellow Wingfoot One and Wingfoot Two which the latter is now home at Wingfoot Lake which is about 25 miles from my home. The front cover of this book shows Wingfoot One as seen from over Mogadore Reservoir while I was kayaking in the summer of 2016.

Many people are not familiar or used to seeing the blimp and there are frequent UFO reports related to it since it is a large cigar shaped object that moves slower than an airplane. Luckily, the folks at Goodyear are quick to respond to emails about the location of the blimp and chances are if there is a major sports event in the area of the sighting the blimp was probably on hand.

Lenticular clouds are the most often misinterpreted cloud for a UFO. These are round shaped clouds that are fairly rare and form around objects which give them their round shape. A majority of these clouds look just like the classic flying saucer shape.

Balloons have historically been misinterpreted as UFOs or have been the cause (Roswell) especially high flying weather balloons. These balloons will stretch and sometimes change shape dramatically as they fly through the atmosphere and are unusual to see so the viewer will more than likely not be able to identify them. There have been a few recent stories of UFOs that turned out to be reflective balloons seen by the eye or filmed with cameras. Google balloons used to bring Internet and phone coverage to remote areas have also been responsible for UFO reports (Abramson).

Chinese lanterns are something that many people might not have seen before. They are typically launched in groups and are separated slightly in elevation but will fly in a loose group. The flame will emit an orange glow and the lantern will go with the flow of the wind and at a distance will look very confusing.

Many countries have sought bans on Chinese lanterns due to a number of problems they create (Westcott). In the United States there are currently 30 states that issue bans on sky or Chinese lanterns due to the fire danger alone (Gabbert). These lanterns are obvious fire hazards since it is essentially a small fire sent adrift with no way to control it. They are responsible for many fires all over the world and are a hazard to not only forests, but also homes, cars, and have even been responsible for burning farm and domestic animals. They can also create false alarms for the Coast Guard as they appear like signal flares in the sky. Chinese lanterns are also an environmental hazard for animals as well as machinery including airplanes. In the citation above by Kathryn Wescott, increases in UFO sightings are included in the article, "Five problems caused by Chinese lanterns".

Drones have become one of the latest issues of UFO sightings. As more drones are flying around one would think we would be used to seeing them, but drones continue to be confused as UFOs or used to fool people into thinking they are UFOs with using an array of odd lights.

Non-physical explanations of UFOs would include **lightning**, electric **transformer explosions, searchlights**, and even **mirages**. These types of explanations fool the viewer into thinking they are seeing a UFO or the effects of a UFO. Some of these are rare occurrences and may not be recognizable by those that are seeing it hence the leap to an unidentified flying object.

Fata morgana is essentially a mirage where objects are seen higher against the horizon than where the objects are. This is similar to when you see a reflection of objects on the road that appear lower than where they really are. While the fata morgana effect of making a ship look like it is flying has been documented for centuries it still confuses people in the 21st century and will be in the news as some odd event every few months or so. These stories are said to be "baffling" or have a "floating city" or other seemingly mysterious object in the sky over or near water and will typically have the explanation of fata morgana accompanying the story.

From these types of explanations we then move to physiological causes. These occur when the body is tricking the mind of the viewer into thinking they are observing a UFO. One effect that is probably at the root of many UFO sightings is pareidolia.

Apophenia is the tendency for people to form patterns from random information. A type of apophenia called pareidolia is where the mind sees random information but perceives it as something recognizable. A lot of focus of pareidolia focuses on the facial recognition aspects of common household items, random lines and shapes, as well as food objects that make people think they see Jesus in toast, a face on Mars, or even the man on the moon.

Pareidolia is a bridge between the physical aspects of false positive UFO sightings and the physiological and psychological aspects. We might see the image of a smiley face, but in reality we are just looking at a large circle with a half circle and two dots. Our minds recognize the familiar pattern and tell us we are seeing a face. This basic example is difficult to see any other way than it being a face at first and this effect can come into play in many other detailed ways that fool us into thinking we are seeing something we are not. The Rorschach inkblot test uses pareidolia to peer into the minds of people based on what they see with random stimuli.

A cloud is a cloud and a lenticular cloud shaped will look like a giant UFO, but, a cloud with dark areas might look like a giant UFO hiding within it. We might capture a bird on video that is closer than it seems be which gives us the impression it might be a UFO (this explanation alone solves a huge percentage of UFO "sightings" during television broadcasts), but a flock of birds tightly grouped may give us the impression that a giant UFO is moving and morphing across the sky and thus is pareidolia.

Another interesting but often ignored physiological issue is the **autokinetic effect** or what is sometimes called **autokinesis**. This is when the eyes are fooled into thinking a stationary object is actually moving especially when the distance between the viewer and the object is unknown. Interestingly, this most often happens with a bright object against a dark object such as a star in the night sky.

It is thought that the autokinetic effect occurs because the eye has little point of reference in certain dark conditions when it has been fixed on a light area. Some, including British psychologist and specialist in human perception Richard Gregory, feel this apparent movement occurs because of movement in the eye which has no frame of reference and the brain is tricked into thinking the object is moving instead (Gregory).

The autokinetic effect has been some concern in the airline industry and military towards pilots. In order to overcome or at least temporarily eliminate the effect it has been suggested to move the gaze away from the light object momentarily and not allow the eyes to stare too long at the object. It is also recommended to gain some sort of fixed frame of reference with the object such as a building to help reduce the illusion of movement. It is also recommended to make even slight head, body, or eye movements to help eliminate this effect (New World Encyclopedia).

What if multiple people see an object move in the sky at night? It is possible that the autokinetic effect can be seen by multiple people at the same time? It's possible as Muzafer Sherif conducted an experiment in 1935 that utilized the autokinetic effect in relation to conformity. He found that when three people guessed the amount of movement the person with the largest discrepancy of the three would conform to the other two in their judgment of the distance the light was purportedly traveling (Sherif). We can certainly expect this type of conformity can and would happen with other types of social situations in judging objects including UFOs.

Conformity is a major issue with UFO believers as it is with a multitude of other topics from politics to religion and the paranormal in general. One major issue is group polarization. This is where the opinions, thoughts, feelings, emotions, and reactions of a group are more strong together than what they would be as private or independently felt by the individuals within the group (Grinnell).

UFO believers are a tight knit group and follow information

about the field very closely. They tend to have some very "out there" reactions to information and beliefs about what is happening with government organizations with cover-ups and even petition with the hope that the government will come clean about all they know through disclosure. I think some people give the government too much credit.

People like to be heard, believed, and people like to feel important. Many labels have been placed on UFO believers and experiencers from fantasy prone personality to having delusions of grandeur, being psychotic (mind not agreeing with reality) and having schizophrenic mental issues.

It is not our focus to determine if someone is lying or if they have one of many mental issues related to those involved in the various aspects of UFO encounters. We should leave that to the professionals and we should not be afraid to tell a potential witness that professional help might allow them understand or cope with what they are feeling about their experience, but never make them feel as though you think they are crazy. And yes, despite the number of things we have covered about what might make someone perceive a UFO with these perceptions cementing their beliefs about the subject it is also possible that the person might just be making things up.

Chapter 3: Trust No One

It was 1989 in London, England. Police were following what appeared to be a large UFO flying slowly through the sky with flashing lights covering its exterior and a bright light at its base. The UFO had been seen by motorists on the M25 that surrounds London. Residents were in a bit of a panic due to the live television reports showing the object descending slowly on the city. Was this an invasion of aliens? The Army had been alerted and was ready to mobilize against this potential threat when the craft went away from London to the county of Surrey and began to land.

Police surrounded the UFO and waited to see what would happen next. A lone officer slowly approached the large UFO when suddenly the door on the craft began to open. Smoke began pouring out of the doorway as everyone watched in awe. To the shock of those watching a short alien walked out from the craft toward the police officer (who subsequently ran in the other direction).

It didn't take too long after this for the story to unfold as an elaborate prank by Richard Branson, a billionaire entrepreneur and the founder of Virgin. Branson was not charged in the prank, but officials were not happy that their resources were tied up that morning (Rojas).

Pranks like this might be a bit harmful, but usually they do not mean to hurt anyone or to create panic only entertain. Hoaxes, on the other hand, are deliberate attempts to fool people by presenting information in a misrepresenting way. UFO hoax videos have become a culture of their own in recent years and a multitude of stories are submitted to UFO and paranormal bloggers that are meant to fool and deceive.

As a UFO researcher and investigator understanding that people will lie is an important thing to understand and accept. Are there real UFO videos on the Internet? Possibly, but the overwhelming amount of misinterpretations and intentional hoaxes have made the Internet an impossible place to trust information especially with video or photographic information without additional data to support them. Any case or photo/video information that is put on the Internet or shared through social media should be highly suspect. What a 15 year old kid can do with video software can rival what a Hollywood studio could produce less than ten years ago on the big screen.

January 4, 2015, a video from Canberra, Australia, shows a landscape at night. In the sky you can see what appear to be the Southern Lights as well as the occasional flicker of lightning. Suddenly, a ball of light begins to form in the sky and becomes brighter and suddenly flashes leaving behind a slowly dimming donut shape in the sky.

The video quickly made the news outlets online as well as the local news in Australia. Australian National University astronomer Brad Tucker stated that he felt that this was ball lightning and even though there should not have been an aurora visible due to very low solar flare activity it might have been caused by the thunderstorm itself.

I was personally a bit shocked by the statement made by the astronomer as I had never heard of a thunderstorm creating an aurora and I found no mention of it anywhere and it also made no sense. He was right that there was no solar flare and reason for the Southern Lights to be active and even if it were it would have been impossible to see with a thunderstorm blowing through the area (which was correct based on historical weather data).

Despite many people believing this was truly ball lightning, especially since the experts said so, I truly felt this was a hoaxed video. Not only was the aurora wrong, but to capture a bright ball of light so perfectly in a camera and not to mention no one else reported seeing this. Still, others thought this might be a wormhole to another dimension or even proof of alien activity on Earth. Then something completely unexpected happened, a man named Johnson Thompson came forward on Reddit and admitted that he had created the video and apologized publicly.

Thompson then created a YouTube video demonstrating how he had created the video just two days after buying Adobe After Effects. He did, however, have experience with Photoshop and other digital effects software that were also used in making the video. He had simply created the video and posted it with the thought that people would realize it was a fake and tell him why (Hill). This public critique would help him become a better digital artist in the future, or so he thought that was how it was going to go.

The holy grail of UFO sightings is to have multiple witnesses report the same sighting. Better yet, multiple witnesses recording clear video of the incident at the same exact time. On January 28, 2011, a pair of videos surfaced from Jerusalem of the Dome of the Rock at Temple Mount, an important religious site, which seemed to show two different views of the same UFO. Not long after a third video of the same event surfaced. Many people took sides quickly as some felt this was definitely proof of UFOs since this was a historic site and the fact that more than one view of the same object were provided.

However, analyzing the story itself a few things seemed highly irregular. First, if this was such a big deal then why were these videos posted anonymously? Why were there no other witnesses to this major sighting over a highly religious and highly populated area and tourist spot? The local media did not seem to have any information about it and all we were left with were the videos.

In the videos we see a large white light descend on the Dome of the Rock. The light sits close to the ground for a few seconds before a bright flash is seen and the UFO flies up and away at an incredible speed. Many people began tearing down the videos as soon as they saw them. The light was not reflecting off of anything, nor was the flash and there was evidence that the video had been used with digital editing software between being filmed and uploaded to YouTube (Radford, 2011b).

Enough evidence began to pile up that more and more people jumped off the bandwagon of belief. It wasn't but a few months later that even MUFON stated that the videos were nothing more than a hoax even though most researchers had moved on already. These videos stand as probably the best series of hoaxed UFO videos to date, but there will certainly be more on the way eventually.

Another type of video hoax that has been on the increase involves advertisers. In late 2015 a series of four photographs and a video came out from Cape Town, South Africa, that centered on a series of sightings of a green UFO. As I was researching the photographs I found that one of them matched a still photo from a video and that was enough for me to deem the whole story as a hoax (Parsons).

It didn't take long, however, for the story to take another turn. As another video came out it was said that it had crashed at a certain location in Cape Town. The video showed the green UFO flying over the city with some cheesy effects of it crashing out of site of the camera. The whole story was heavily tied to social media which made a lot of sense when it was revealed what was behind the story. This ended up being a viral campaign for an energy drink that wanted people to come out to the location to sample the new product.

Many of the UFO videos on YouTube and many paranormal blogs center on ones seen in space with the International Space Station or from other missions in space. The Mars Exploration

Rovers (Spirit, Opportunity, and Curiosity) have also been a major focus as photographs are constantly being said to contain aliens or other objects that should not be on Mars that "prove" that aliens are on the planet.

The focus here is that the government and NASA are lying about what is going on out there. The reality is that these videos are misinterpretations or are purposely hoaxed videos.

It's hard as a researcher or investigator to have to deal with all of these purported UFO videos. Believe me, as I research for my show the *Paranormal News Insider* each week I see a number of these videos from ghosts to cryptids and UFOs and an overwhelming majority are easily and quickly explained or dismissed. On one hand it's hard to want to get roped in to such nonsense when you already know it's probably going to be either a misinterpretation or hoax. But, on the other hand it's hard to ignore some potential evidence or a big story that might be breaking.

The key to dealing with videos, photographs, and stories dealing with purported UFO evidence is to be skeptical and not be drawn into it emotionally. For many when they do see these videos they are either quick to say "real" or "hoax". So often you will read the comments area of a YouTube video or a story and you will see grand debates over details of the video or people arguing that it is real or fake based on their beliefs or other information that has nothing to do with what is involved with the particular story.

With these pieces of information we should always be on guard and look for the things that make no sense or that will expose the story as not true as a hoax or misinterpretation. The most dangerous thing we can do is assume anything about the photo, video, or story one way or the other until we can examine various parts of it to look for inconsistencies.

I will talk in more detail about what to look for when it comes to videos and photographs as well as the stories that peddle them to help solve them in the chapter in Part III with researching.

Chapter 4: The Six Keys to Success

I have conducted many presentations at various ghost, Bigfoot, and even UFO events where I talked about a variety of information concerning many aspects of the paranormal and how to research and investigate. I try very hard to speak to the variety of people who are in attendance to these events and a few years ago I created a slide that talked about six keys to being a good ghost investigator. These were just generalized statements that I used to relate to the field and how some simple understanding could help create a solid foundation of knowledge and experience in the ghost field.

I realized that these keys could be applied to the other paranormal fields and potentially to other aspects of life as well. I have since used these six keys to success in other presentations for cryptozoology and with UFOs. These six keys are not meant to simplify what it takes to be a researcher or investigator in the anomalous fields as it takes a lot more knowledge and experience than many people are willing to admit. This oversimplification merely serves as a way to reach people on a different level than being overly technical and especially with the limited amount of time during a presentation at a conference, convention, or other event.

The six keys to success are just basic ideas of how to look at these fields objectively. We have talked a lot about photographs, videos, perception, stories, misinformation, and many other topics that create the foundation for UFO research and investigation. As we get ready to move to the section on casework I want to provide some general information that can help put UFO research or even other fields into a simple perspective.

1. **Know what is normal** – Until you know what is normal how can you say what is abnormal or even paranormal? If you're not familiar with watching large jets in holding patterns, approach and takeoff, or flying at you it would be difficult to discern what you are seeing at great distances. Obviously most of us are familiar with seeing jets and airplanes, but what about Chinese lanterns or drones? Are you familiar with seeing a meteor entering the atmosphere or seeing the International Space Station float overhead? Just knowing what can cause the various sightings is a critical step in understanding UFO cases. Being able to know that a great blue heron or other large bird might be responsible for a person seeing a low flying UFO over a reservoir is a pretty good deduction, but you have to know when and where these and other large birds might be. It takes a bit of knowledge of the everyday world around us and what might happen in certain locations. Chinese lanterns might be released in any residential neighborhood, but the Goodyear blimp frequents large sporting events, and rocket launches and meteor sightings can be easily researched. You just have to know they are there and where to look to find the information.

2. **No substitute for experience** – This goes along with the first item. It is important to know what is

out there but it is also important to get to get the experience of seeing these things for your own familiarity. Understanding what things look like in the sky and being able to recognize them is very important as an investigator if you are going to observe a location where someone has seen something strange. This experience will also help you if you are talking to a client and they are describing something to you that might ring a bell from your experience. Being able to quickly interpret a red or green blinking light on an airplane or jet, knowing what a satellite looks like or when you should be able to see them are great experiences to have. Having a good understanding of space, science, airplanes, as well as the physiological and psychological things I mentioned in the last chapter should be something to have knowledge and experience in as well. No UFO researcher should lack experience in stargazing or observing the night sky and attempting to identify things they are seeing. It is good practice to do this in your own neighborhood but also to practice when you are on vacation or in an unfamiliar location. Observing things and figuring out what they are provide excellent experience in helping others figure out what they are seeing as well as visualizing what the client is describing.

3. **Interview early and often** – We will cover the interview process in depth in a few chapters. Many people want to just jump in to cases and are only concerned about the big details about sightings. However, minor information about when, where, what, and how are just not enough to dig into the client's belief or understanding about what they think they saw. Interviewing might not be your strong suit but it is an important facet of being an investigator and a researcher. When first receiving a case try to get a phone number or be able to meet the client in

person as soon as possible regardless of how long ago the sighting was. Interviewing the person as early as possible will also help you in your research and investigation and will get you out in front of a case since the person may have contacted other people. There are other reasons for interviewing early that we will discuss later, but interviewing often is another key facet in gathering information. Any time you have a question or need more information contact the client and ask for clarity. Retouching parts of the interview can allow the client to provide more details they might have forgotten to initially tell you or will allow them to further expand on with your contact.

4. **Do your research** – Researching various details of a case might seem time consuming, but digging in to specific pieces of a case are what helps solve them. It is critical that we examine all possibilities for sightings before assuming that there is no explanation or that an alien space ship is responsible for a sighting. Breaking a case down into pieces also helps keep our assumptions and beliefs from getting in the way. Research might come from websites, books, calling a local airport, university, observatory, or even shopping in the area to find things that might fit the description of what the witness might have seen. It is not merely sitting behind your computer or scrolling with your phone. You will have to dig for information or reach out to another researcher or an expert in a specific field at times; it's just what we have to do. As with ghosts and cryptids it might seem like the best way to solve things is get out to where the person saw something and hope you can have a repeat performance. However, you will have far better luck if you attempt to look at the individual pieces of data that you have collected from an interview, a site survey, documenting photographs, and any evidence collected by you or the client

(photographs, video, etc.). Granted, observation of the location during the day and night are also great ways to conduct research as well as to physically investigate the location.

5. **Be objective (assume nothing)** – It is nearly impossible to be completely objective when dealing with a field case or a subject like UFOs. However, you should do your best not to let emotions, beliefs, or opinions get in the way of helping with a case. This really helps when you first communicate with a potential client. You don't want to tell them you believe what they saw was definitely a UFO. This might be a great way to bond at first, but when you figure out what they saw was just the planet Venus that explanation won't go over as well as it would had you told them that you will allow the evidence to speak for itself in advance. In many cases researchers and investigators make assumptions about the case from when they first talk to the witness to when they see photographs or other evidence. Being objective is important so you can see everything without preconceived notions and when your emotions and beliefs come in to play you will begin to have assumptions about the case. Once you go down this path you will have blinders on and will not be able to see the entirety of the case.

6. **Solve the mystery** – The interview, photographs, measurements, investigation, research, and all of the other pieces of the overall case can be tiresome to collect, research, and interpret. The bottom line is that you are merely trying to figure out the most likely reason behind what the person saw. Don't become distracted from trying to prove that UFOs or other facets of the field exist or get caught up in other things outside of merely putting the pieces of the puzzle together. Also, don't get caught up in minor details of the case you are investigating. Be

able to stand back and look at the bigger picture with the case, but not the bigger picture of the field or trying to validate something or gain publicity or notoriety. If you just focus on gathering information, identifying potential explanations and disseminating the facts your work will quickly speak for itself. Don't view it as you are trying to figure out exactly what was in the sky at this particular time and throw everything against the wall to see what sticks or try and overcomplicate the case by thinking of it as specifically a UFO case. The key is to just try and put the facts together to see what fits and view it as merely solving a mystery of the most logical explanation. The evidence should dictate direction and you must allow the data to do the talking and allow it to go wherever it needs to.

Part III: Casework: Investigation and Research

Chapter 1: UFO, MUFON, SETI, *and other Acronyms of Research*

The word "UFO" typically creates the image of a flying saucer piloted by short aliens with big eyes in many people's heads. To some it might mean a strange light high in the sky that moves in ways that seem to defy logical explanation. As we have learned so far there are many things that are attached to the UFO culture, but what is a UFO really?

The term UFO, Unidentified Flying Object, actually started out abbreviated as UFOB. This acronym was created not by UFOlogists or other anomalous researchers, but by the United States Air Force. The term is defined in the Air Force Regulation 200-2 (AFR 200-2). In a memo dated August 12, 1954 the Air

Force defined a UFOB:

> "Unidentified Flying Objects (UFOB) relates to any airborne object which by performance, aerodynamic characteristics, or unusual features, does not conform to any presently known aircraft or missile type, or which cannot be positively identified as a familiar object."

A copy of this regulation is available on the CUFON (The Computer UFO Network) website at http://www.cufon.org/cufon/afr200-2.htm.

The Air Force definition essentially goes beyond the typical "if I can't tell what it is then it's a UFO" types of definitions that are repeated by many in the field, but it is also careful to avoid stating they are from another planet. Unfortunately, UFO culture has made both of these concepts synonymous and you will not get one without the other.

Dictionary.com defines a UFO as "Any unexplained moving object observed in the sky, especially one assumed by some observers to be of extraterrestrial origin." The Oxford English Dictionary says a UFO is, "A mysterious object seen in the sky for which it is claimed no orthodox scientific explanation can be found, often supposed to be a vehicle carrying extraterrestrials." Cambridge Dictionary states, "Abbreviation for unidentified flying object (= an object seen in the sky that some people believe is a spacecraft from another planet)." Macmillan Dictionary says, "An unidentified flying object: a strange object that flies through the sky that no one can recognize. Some people think UFOs are a sign of life on other planets."

Dr. Carl Sagan, an astronomer, astrobiologist, astrophysicist, cosmologist, author, and a believer in life in outer space, defined a UFO as:

> "Unidentified flying objects (UFOs) [are] the generic term for moving aerial or celestial phenomena, detected visually or by radar, whose nature is not immediately understood. Interest in these objects stems from speculation that some of them are the products of civilizations beyond the earth, and from the psychological insights into contemporary human problems that

this interpretation, provides."

So, again, we have the "not sure what it could be" statement and the "it's probably from outer space" connection as well. Unfortunately, as much as I have always said that a UFO merely means something we can't initially identify in the sky the culture has become a two headed monster that we cannot ignore. You will  never be able to merely refer to a UFO as just "something I can't easily identify" without the "alien" part attached. This concept has become part of the definition over time and has become entrenched in the culture of UFOs worldwide. It has become a large coin. There are two sides to every coin and while you may prefer heads there will always be tails and nothing you do can separate the two. However, Dr. Sagan also brought up an interesting point about using the term UFO to describe the variety of objects described in reports.

"Unidentified flying objects have been described variously as rapidly moving or hovering; disc-shaped, cigar-shaped, or ball-shaped; moving silently or noisily; with a fiery exhaust or with no exhaust whatever; accompanied by flashing lights, or uniformly glowing with a silvery cast. The diversity of the observations suggests that UFO's have no common origin and that the use of such terms as UFO's or "flying saucers" serves only to confuse the issue by grouping generically a variety of unrelated phenomena." (Sagan).

This last observation that sticking a generic label on the variety of sightings leads me to my next thought. UFO sightings are generally categorized by shape (sphere, triangle, saucer, etc.), but we do not look past this other than for statistical purposes. When we think of UFOs we think of the craft and their potential for being created by extraterrestrials. We also think that the investigation of UFOs is attempting to figure out what was in the sky. The reality is, we are not investigating the UFO we are actually investigating the witness and their testimony (Glenday).

I had initially wanted to title this book, *Handbook for the Amateur*

UFOlogist, just as my prior books were geared toward amateur paranormal investigators, ghost hunters, and cyrptozoologists. While UFOlogy is essentially "the study of UFOs" the focus of UFOlogy is essentially on figuring out what UFOs are and if there is really any evidence hidden by governments around the world. Instead of waiting on "disclosure" and lump all UFO reports together I would rather separate them for what they are- individual reports of distinct sightings. Not to mention that some people may read "UFOlogist" as urologist and we have enough people in the field engaging in contests of going back and forth similar to what these latter "ologists" might ask a sample of for study.

Another way to think about it is this. The evidence and data created by the case will give us the best chance to define what the witness saw. If we go into a case with the assumption that a "UFO" was involved, no matter what fancy definition we settle on, the assumption has been made that the craft is from another world or even a "top secret project" that ultimately leads to government conspiracies and UFOs from other planets.

If we are just UFOlogists (or even UFO researchers I suppose) the craft is technically no longer a UFO. If we arrive with the supposition that it is a UFO, potential alien craft, we have already identified what it is and it is technically no longer an Unidentified Flying Object! I know, it is a dizzying conundrum, but it is something that the culture of UFO research has created. So, what else do we call this then?

Technically, the study of UFOs in the context of them being alien controlled spacecraft is called saucerology. Again, if the assumption is made that the craft is from alien technology then we have essentially identified it at least to a certain extent. This thought process goes hand in hand with the last chapter of Part II. In this chapter I talked about the six keys to success with the last one being solve the mystery. We can't let terminology get in the way of how we intend to dismantle and research any topic. We also certainly do not want it to influence those that are seeing these things into thinking that there are only two potential outcomes to their sighting; explainable or aliens.

Now that we have defined a UFO let's look at the groups that have investigated and researched them other than government programs. The Aerial Phenomena Research Organization (APRO) was formed in 1952 in Wisconsin and grew to having many state branches and representatives in many countries over the years. The organization had many scientists involved with it and educated experts in various areas (anatomy, biochemistry, biophysics, botany, astronomy, geology, physics, psychology, and more) with a PhD (Ruhl).

In 1969 the Midwest UFO Network grew out of members of APRO. As MUFON grew beyond the Midwest and began to gain worldwide representation it changed its name, but kept its acronym, to the Mutual UFO Network (Schuessler). In 1988 APRO ceased to exist. MUFON currently boasts over 4,000 members worldwide.

The National Investigations Committee on Aerial Phenomena (NICAP) was formed in late 1956 and by the early 1960s boasted over 14,000 members. The group was not without its issues as it had encountered financial problems just prior to the boom in interest in UFOs and the extra membership. Later that decade membership dropped, mostly due to the Condon Report, and it never stopped culminating in the end of NICAP by 1980.

The Center for UFO Studies (CUFOS) started in 1973 and was founded by J Allen Hynek who served as a consultant for Project Blue Book. Although Hynek died in 1986 CUFOS lives on as an archival and investigative organization based in the United States.

There are many other active and inactive groups in the United States and all over the world with that had or have a focus on a particular area of research. MUFON continues to be the largest U.S. organization and gathers more cases than any other worldwide organization. One could argue that despite many people thinking that the government is hiding secrets and is one big conspiracy theory of hidden information, the rash of a number of UFO reporting and investigating communities worldwide kept these reports from landing on the desk of the U.S. Air Force. Could these groups really be the perpetrators of hidden or missing information? It might not be any of the acronymic entities intentions, but such a hypothesis should be considered that spreading this information out thinly might have curbed the Air Force's data stream and caused them to shut down their projects and ignore the phenomena.

SETI, the Search for Extraterrestrial Intelligence, began as a term used for any organization that searched for signs of life in outer space. In 1984 the SETI Institute was created that focused a multitude of projects (135 multiyear projects) that have been funded and conducted by NASA, other government entities, as well as private corporations. SETI is widely known for its SETI@Home project where users allow their computers to crunch data looking for unique signals in space.

SETI focuses on potential signals from outer space that hopefully come from intelligent beings. That's it. There is no focus on potential UFOs visiting Earth as well as the multiple limiting factors behind sending and receiving any type of signal from space. Stanton Friedman, the voice behind many aspects of UFO belief has said the SETI should actually stand for Silly Effort To Investigate (Friedman).

On the flipside of SETI there is METI which stands for Messaging to Extra-Terrestrial Intelligence or known as Active SETI. METI is about sending signals into space typically in the form of radio signals. METI, like SETI, began as a mere concept but is now an organization that focuses on both messaging and receiving. Physicist Stephen Hawking has addressed his fears over the years since 2010 that he is a bit fearful of alien contact for a few reasons as mentioned earlier in this book. "If aliens visit us, the outcome would be much as when Columbus landed in America, which didn't turn out well for the Native Americans. We only have to look at ourselves to see how intelligent life might develop into something we wouldn't want to meet" (Heussner).

Many attack SETI and METI since they feel they are ignoring the data that is all around them. There are so many UFO reports, so how can they ignore this? In all honesty, one of the biggest issues with METI and SETI is the overwhelming odds that a signal could be sent or received with detection methods in the right place at the right time, enough strength to be picked up at all, and the ability to discern the message sent.

One of the best books on this topic in my opinion was written by Professor Antonio Paris. Paris recently potentially solved the near 40 year question of what caused the Wow! signal by determining that a comet was more than likely the cause of the 1420 MHz signal detected near the Sagittarius constellation in 1977 at the Big Ear Radio Telescope in Delaware, Ohio (Paris). For years this was the big bragging point of SETI, but now the startling reality of the complexity and near impossibility of such signals is coming into focus.

In his book, "Space Science", Paris discusses many aspects about space that brings the UFO reality down to Earth quickly. Our first signal shot into space on purpose toward the constellation Hercules in late 1974 was a hallmark idea when it happened. Unfortunately, the area the signal was aimed at will more than likely have moved by the time the signal reaches it in 25,000 years and the signal would be so weak it probably wouldn't be picked up especially if "they" are using advanced technology and wouldn't be concerned with such "ancient" methods. The signal dilemma is also looked at as the likelihood that another civilization could understand the message or that it is a message at all would be slim.

Paris also outlines the vastness of space and the inherent dangers of interstellar travel. After reading this book you will definitely feel very small and very lonely as you realize that space travel as we perceive it is nowhere near the reality that it is. Being a tiny speck in the Milky Way galaxy we can see things in the sky that would be a near impossibility to reach due to the physical, physiological, and psychological dangers that are often dismissed or ignored in UFO research circles as well as in the cultural influences all around us.

As you can see from this sample there are many organizations that are (or have been) investigating UFOs and related information in various ways. Granted, I have not mentioned crop circle or other facets that are related to UFOs which have their own organizations geared toward research and documentation.

We have seen governmental attempt to determine whether

UFOs are a threat to national security to non-profit organizations that grew from a region in the United States to worldwide organizations that investigate cases as they appear. With so many organizations worldwide focusing on so many various approaches one would think the UFO answer would have been solved by now.

Part of the issue is that these private organizations operate as businesses and are not as selective as they should be with those who participate in the group. This has led to many issues from financial mishandling (NICAP) to being accused of being part of the cover-up (MUFON), not following set forth protocol in case investigation methods and reinforcing the pseudoscience label for UFOlogy (MUFON) among many other issues.

However, these surviving groups are all that we have as far as large eyes and ears dedicated to investigating and researching the many facets of UFOs. If I've painted a grim picture of UFO research and reality it is not done on purpose. What I am doing with this book is trying to bring the reality into focus so that we can investigate this phenomenon with clear eyes and a truly open mind to the realistic limitations of the subject matter. So, what are you going to do?

Chapter 2: Becoming a Researcher and Investigator

The field of UFOs seems to rely heavily on those that research. Researching might mean sifting through old documents or tracking down and interviewing witnesses or knowledgeable people in specific areas to solidify leads on specific details. A researcher is one who systematically reviews a subject looking to discover new leads or create theories on what truly happened with various circumstances. Although definitions for both words are fairly similar I view an investigator as someone who gathers information or data specifically in the field with direct evidence or through the witness.

I view a researcher as one who makes sense of the information or data and allows it to tell a story. The researcher is also the one who comes up with information for the investigator to, well, investigate. It is essentially a symbiotic relationship since nothing can make sense if there is no information coming in and if there is no one to disseminate data or determine what direction to go in next the collection process of an investigation is meaningless.

Granted, a researcher and investigator can be the same person and hopefully with you it will be, but they are two distinct roles that must be performed to allow a case to flow correctly. Again, they are technically the same thing, but I like to view these two areas as a little more overlapping than "lab work" (research) and field work (investigation) especially since we all do both sometimes simultaneously. Unfortunately, not much usually comes in the way of actual physical evidence to investigate, but that does not mean we have to sit at our desks and throw pencils into the ceiling while waiting on a case.

The act of interviewing a client, investigating the scene of the sighting, and researching the data gathered at the scene are fairly involved for anyone at any level of experience. But, factor in some of the more "fringy" subjects that you might have to deal with and you might change your mind about getting into this field. Just as in the ghost field and cryptozoology field, there are no such things as "typical" cases in UFO research.

Granted, as someone who researches anomalous topics you can pick and choose what types of cases you want to pursue. I would recommend sticking to UFO sightings for a while. You will get the occasional photograph or video sent your way that won't be so much about solving a case but figuring out the details of the evidence, but I would recommend staying away from abduction and contactee cases. These types of cases can become quite complicated due to the potential issues you might run into with those that sometimes display these types of experiences. There is really no way to "solve" these types of cases and generally these people just want an audience.

This book is just a primer and there is a lot more you will need to learn as well as experience in order to become a more rounded researcher and investigator. Working with someone in the field with more knowledge and/or experience than you is always recommended, but finding a mentor is not always easy. Anyone in a field that lacks a formal education process should do their best to learn new things within and outside the field to compliment the things they know or need to know to become more successful at solving mysteries.

Those with a background in police work, interviewing, social work, psychology, and even retail can help as these deal with communication with people as well as potentially helping people problem solve. A background in a scientific discipline would also be a great help to a potential UFO researcher or investigator especially in astronomy, physics, or even surveying.

Probably the biggest reality is that you will more than likely not make a living at being a UFO researcher. One of the biggest debates in the ghost field is over charging clients. A majority of groups feel that this is the worst thing in the world and will frequently attack those that do verbally in social media. While part of me thinks that this will weed out cases where people are pranking or using it for attention it will not be overly affective to charge people for merely attempting to solve a mystery of a sighting for them. There aren't many, if any, people that get paid to travel the world investigating UFO sightings and most people will make less money writing several books than they would if they shoveled the neighbors walk for a few months in the winter.

That being said, there is no formal academic degree in anything to do with UFOs. However, there are plenty of places to learn about UFOs but slightly less that will teach you how to investigate them. One online university I would highly recommend is the Institute of Metaphysical Humanistic Science. IMHS can provide you a degree in UFOlogy that will enhance your knowledge of a variety of aspects of the field including investigating cases, leading your own group, and understand how to deal with people. I graduated from IMHS with my bachelor's degree in metaphysical science in 2012 and then my master's and PhD in late 2013 and thoroughly enjoyed my journey through the coursework. Find more information at http://www.metaphysicsinstitute.org/program-info/specializations/ufology.

I would also highly recommend the sister school to IMHS which is Thomas Francis University. Through TFU you can earn a degree in UFOlogy or merely take individual courses on various topics and always get your degree later if you desire. Find more information about Thomas Francis University at http://www.tfuniversity.org/.

Once you decide to get into the field and try and solve some cases you will have a few choices as to how you are going to do this. One option already mentioned would be to find someone who could mentor you and guide you through cases potentially one-on-one or through a group setting including MUFON which I will discuss in a moment. Again, this is not always the easiest thing to make happen, but I would highly recommend finding someone who is willing to show you the ropes or at least give you some guidance until you learn what you can or while taking courses or obtaining a degree.

An option I would recommend is being an independent researcher and investigator. As an independent researcher you can work alone or ask others in various areas to assist you when needed. These "others" might include ghost groups you might know that have a good interviewer or access to recording equipment you do not have. The goal with networking is to work with someone or a group of people that can offer you something you do not have or need in a particular case. If you are not overly comfortable with interviewing then bringing along someone who is will obviously benefit you. Bringing in these others will also benefit them if they have a desire to be involved with a UFO case, granted, you will have to take charge of the case if it is yours and be the lead in the case even if the others are pitching in and doing a lot of work.

The major downside to going it alone is that it is highly recommended, if not absolutely necessary in some circumstances, to bring at least one person along with you to a case. There is plenty of danger that comes with investigating and not a lot of it comes from UFOs or aliens. Most investigators in the anomalous fields will agree that it isn't ghosts or Bigfoot they are afraid of; it's the regular living people that scare you or make you feel extremely uncomfortable in certain situations.

I have had plenty of cases where I had a strong feeling that one or more of the clients were intoxicated or under the influence of a drug of some sort. In more than one case I was put into the situation of having to become a family mediator since it seemed that the ghost case was nothing more than a front for bringing in a complete stranger to help them with their family communication problems.

In more than one of these cases I was absolutely alone as an investigator. In one case another investigator was supposed to meet me at the location, but had an emergency for which she did not bother to contact me. It was a very long and nerve wracking night for me to say the least and I was very close to calling the police as I felt that they were not going to let me leave the house until I solved their personal problems. I and the other investigator had a feeling that something was up with the family before heading out and we had both agreed to wait for the other, but I drove by the home and one of the clients was outside smoking near the street and directed me to the home. I think the thing that really helped was the fact that I had a recorder in my pocket with a lapel microphone the entire time. Needless to say, that was the last case where I ever went in alone and the last time I didn't do at least a little background research on a potential client.

When jumping into the fray of UFO cases you might not get a lot even when putting out a website, a Facebook site, and other online methods. As stated in the last chapter there are many organizations that operate worldwide which are competing for cases. Many ghost groups have become tired of the "ghost scene" and have moved into the cryptozoology and UFO area which causes further competition. This competition is not necessarily a bad thing as it forces groups and individuals to become the best of the best in order to acquire casework.

Other than striking it out alone another easy option is for you to join a group. Joining a group once you gain some knowledge and experience can help get you to your next personal level. If you decide to join a group it will also mean following someone else's protocol and methodology. Adhering to someone else's way of doing things isn't necessarily a bad thing since it can teach you a lot as well as help you form good habits of investigating cases. Granted, it could also the exact opposite of this so get a good feel for if this will be a mutually beneficial fit before committing.

The biggest group to join would be that of MUFON. The Mutual UFO Network is the largest group in the United States that is focused on researching and investigating new and historical cases. MUFON offers a lot in the way of educating you and allowing you to investigate in your own area since it is made up of state chapters.

However, all states are not the same as far as communication and the opportunity to go out on an investigation. To become an investigator for MUFON you have to be a member and some of the expenses such as the Field Investigator's Manual can be quite expensive. Also, MUFON is large and is a non-profit organization and is not immune to internal and external conflict caused by leadership.

You may also consider creating your own group. One might consider this an extension to working alone although you can create your own group and others will follow your lead. Unfortunately, operating an anomalous research team isn't always as easy as finding like-minded people and going out on investigations together. The best thing about running your own group is that you are in charge. The worst thing about running your own group is that you are in charge.

There is quite a bit that goes into fielding a successful anomalous research team. The biggest thing about operating your own group is that you are in charge of nurturing it into something successful and putting together the pieces that will lead it in that direction. Oh, and it's a lot of work not just to build but to maintain. This might sound like a pain that isn't worth it, but it is great to run your own group as long as things are going good.

One of the most important things which is usually overlooked is a code of ethics. A code of ethics outlines how you will act and what your beliefs are toward specific topics such as how quickly you commit to getting in touch with a client (24 hours or less hopefully) or other aspects that outline your professionalism toward being a group with strong morals. As simple as it sounds a code of ethics lays the foundation for the group's focus and approach. Most paranormal groups fail because of a cohesive lack of focus.

Also a smart idea is to create standards and protocols. Standards and protocols are an extension of the code of ethics essentially outlining how the group will conduct itself with a mission, goal, and how you approach casework in the field with specifics broken down into sections. This will provide a written outline of how the group will conduct investigations, interact with the public, what beliefs are common within the group, how members should act toward the public and each other, how evidence is collected, processed, researched, and reviewed, and so on. For an example of a detailed standards and protocols feel free to check out one I helped create for a group that I am Co-Director for which is Ohio Anomalous Research (https://tinyurl.com/yaaojxr5).

Also remember that if you are going to create a team you will have to have some leadership skills. Describing what it takes to be a good leader could easily fill a book or ten, but some easy advice would be that you have to be clear and timely with communication with your members as well as your potential clients. You have to be willing to make tough decisions such as telling someone they are not a good fit for your team to tough discussions like telling someone they are no longer a member of your team (no one said this would be easy).

Communication also means coordinating meetings, arrival times to investigations, creating other ways to keep members engaged such as sky watches, frequently updating a website or social media, or even delegating some or all of these functions to the members within the group. Along with delegation is follow up. Following up on someone is making sure they are getting things done without them thinking you don't trust them to complete their task. It is also to make sure they understand it and are doing in a way that will be more than satisfactory to your tastes.

As the leader it will be up to you to direct and provide motivation for others to continually improve their own personal skills as well as be involved with the group. Keeping people actively involved has always been one of the issues I have encountered with operating a paranormal group. A UFO group will not just meet to investigate cases, but should also have frequent meetings in person at least once a month. Online meetings are also beneficial since they can fit in easier with schedules, but there is little substitute for actually being physically in front of each other. Between cases or when cases are infrequent a sky watch would be a great way to get individuals involved. A sky watch would merely be finding a dark and quiet place to observe the sky. With this activity you can be able to observe stars, planets, satellites, and other phenomena in order to gain the experience or teach others what they are observing.

Another subject that I want to touch on before jumping into the investigation aspect is that of equipment. For ghost groups it is thought that the more tools and Pelican cases they own the more serious they will be taken by other groups and clients and it means that they know what they are doing. To me, a lot of tools mean that the group is reliant upon the tech to provide them answers or they have allowed themselves to believe that the technology is necessary in order to conduct investigations. For UFOlogy it doesn't seem to be the issue.

While ghost groups rely on EMF detectors it is interesting to note that they were used in UFO research long before. An EMF detector is not a necessity for UFO research in my opinion, but having one to determine logical sources of high readings might help with ongoing hallucinations of a client.

Cameras, binoculars, and potentially telescopes should be a staple for anyone who intends to document as well as observe things at a distance. Cameras are an absolute necessity in order to document the location at various angles as well as to document the collection of any potential evidence at the scene. Binoculars come in handy to spot while investigating a case as well as with a sky watch or any other activity outside. On the flipside, I would also recommend carrying a magnifying glass to help enlarge smaller objects or look for details within objects that may be potential evidence at the scene.

Flashlights are also a staple for any person that intends to be outside at night. I highly recommend having at least one strong flashlight in your arsenal (at least 200 lumens) as well as having one with a red lens which helps preserve night vision.

Audio recorders and well as video recorders are a nice addition to conducting interviews. Always get permission prior to recording a client with audio or video. Recording an interview serves many purposes with documenting what is said to being able to review and have others directly observe or hear what was said.

There are plenty of other tools that UFO groups employ such as radiation meters or Geiger counters. While these are great to have in case of a UFO landing or crash case they would more than likely be a waste of money overall. If the time comes where you need one there are usually places where you can rent them although you should understand how any piece of equipment works before attempting to use it in an active case.

Physical evidence collection would be a dream come true for any UFO researcher, but it will be rare if ever that you will come across a piece of an alien craft or something affected by radiation. However, as rare as this is you want to be at least minimally prepared in case it happens. Having vinyl or rubber gloves on hand (pun intended) is a good idea (NEVER touch anything you think is evidence with anything that is living including poking it with a stick). Bags of various sizes including zip lock bags are not a bad idea to carry all the time as well.

Always keep at least a foot long ruler as well as a medium to large size measuring tape with you every time you go out to a case in order to measure or document the size of something in a photograph. Always document your evidence collection method with photographs at every step (no matter how many photographs you have to take) or with video. Also, always mark your evidence bags with the date, time, location, as well as who collected the information as well as how it was documented. If you are using any bag other than a zip lock bag seal it with tape before leaving the scene. If the evidence is given to someone else other than who collected it document this transfer with the date and time of transfer on the bag as well as document in your notes. I will discuss this in more detail in a later chapter in this section.

Last, but certainly not least, you should have a way of documenting everything that happens during a case (other than audio/video). Maintaining a log of events will come in handy if you actually do find something interesting or a case lasts several weeks or months. This can be as simple as a notebook to as complicated as laptop or using your phone. I would recommend whatever is easiest for you to maintain in a file for dissemination or for others to see if in a group setting. Always document every step of any investigation especially if you are collecting something from the scene.

Another aspect to being a good researcher is to establish contacts. Establishing contacts in UFO research is critical since a majority of cases happen once, but happen in areas where other people may have observed them and might have even reported them to someone else. Knowing other researchers in your state or local area is important as well as having established some sort of working relationship with them when you begin taking cases.

Reaching out to law enforcement agencies for cases in your local area might sound a bit scary, maybe for fear they will lock you up, but many police departments will not waste their time investigating these reports and may readily hand them over to you. You should also at least have the contact information for local municipal and regional airports. If you need information for flights you can look up historical information online through flight tracking websites for larger craft, but smaller craft you will have to resort to contacting the smaller local airports. It's not a bad idea to have a map and have all of these locations noted in advance as well for reference in your general vicinity.

Before making this decision to start a group, join a group, or strike it out on your ow you should feel comfortable with the areas covered in this book including the interview section that is coming in the next chapter. Interviewing seems to be the one thing that few people want to do. It might sound great to just "get out there", but an interview can tell you a tremendous amount of detail behind what might be going on and "getting out there" isn't always necessary.

Chapter 3: The Interview Process

People make horrible witnesses. We have all heard this. Since 1989, 350 people have been exonerated of crimes through the use of DNA evidence and of these cases 71% of them involved eyewitness identification (Innocence Project). So, does that mean we should never trust what anyone says they see?

These statistics and the mentality behind people being bad witnesses is a little misunderstood. The fact is it's not people's minds or memories that are always bad but are sometimes mislead. These facts and figures I've mentioned come from crimes and convictions. During the process of investigations and court cases a person's memory can become malleable, in other words the testimony can be contorted by police during a lineup or by a lawyer during cross examination. If proper protocol of the statement of an eyewitness were followed it could be viewed as reliable as DNA evidence in a crime (Wixted, Mickles).

This fact plays an importance in how we interact with a client during the course of the UFO investigation. First, we must respond right away to their initial request to discuss information about the case. An email conversation should be the last method of continued contact and an immediate phone call should take place. This first contact is important since we need to document what the client has to say about what happened as soon as possible before they tell the story too many times or are influenced by other people's thoughts and opinions.

Second, keep your opinions about what might have been seen by the client to yourself. Do not agree with any of the suggestions the client may give you for what they feel it might have been as this is the same as telling them what you think. The key is to be objective and keep from influencing the client. The client is your main piece of evidence and contaminating it should be the last thing you want to do if you desire a legitimate investigation of what happened.

If the case is a recent one you will want to schedule a face to face interview as soon as possible. A face to face interview will allow you more time, less distraction, and to get a more solid feel for the description of the case by directly observing the client and being able to interact with them. A historical sighting (many months or years ago) or one that the client merely wants to report but isn't confident about may not need to be pursued immediately or at all.

The client has agreed to meet you and is eager to give you the finer details of their sighting. Be sure the client understands the interview is an important aspect of the investigation and be sure to let them know it could take at least an hour or more to conduct properly. Also be sure that the interview is conducted in a location that can offer privacy and be free of distractions. Granted, if meeting in a local restaurant this might be difficult, just try to avoid meal times and ask the client if they feel comfortable in discussing the subject in depth in that setting. It's usually not impossible to find a seating location that has some distance from other patrons as well as foot traffic for a bit of privacy.

The client should only invite those that are pertinent to the sighting unless it is a spouse or close friend that is there to support them, especially in a case where you are male and they are female or vice versa. This information should be communicated prior to the interview. Keeping unnecessary people away from the interview and investigation will help speed up the process and minimize contamination and distractions during both processes. Many times someone who knows of the sighting may feed the original witness information and this will be very unproductive.

They should also be in the right frame of mind to conduct an interview. Are they stressed or scared about what happened? Do they seem nervous about the interview or investigation? Distracted by work, television, children, or something else? Politely remind them that they contacted you and you are here on your own time to help them with this issue. Redirecting people will typically be easy, just remember to be direct but polite!

The same needs to be true with you as well. Don't update your Facebook status, reply to text messages, or even have your phone on. Don't take smoke breaks until the interview is complete or until the client needs a break. Remember, you are also there at their request so respect their time as much as you desire them to respect yours.

Before beginning the interview be sure to ask if they will give their permission to record the conversation. This also should be asked prior to the interview, but always ask prior to actually pulling out a recorder as this surprise may not be taken well. A regular digital recorder will work just fine. This should be done as a reference tool so that no details will be missed. The information should be confidential and a basic confidentiality form (and potentially a liability form on private property to free them from responsibility if you were to get hurt on their property by accident) should be prepared in advance to let them know that you will not use any information about the case without their permission as well as let them know that they are not to use the evidence you gather for personal gain either (writing a book, being on the news, etc.) without your permission.

You will also want to let the client know that you will be using a structured interview and will be guiding them through the process. Creating and controlling an interview will help it become quicker and you will gather a lot more information from it. If you just ask someone to describe what they saw and merely fill out a questionnaire you will be missing a lot of the story. Having structure to your interview as well as your investigation shows confidence in what you are doing and will surely persuade the client that you know what you are doing.

Lastly, let them know you will be asking some tough questions and may sound at times that you doubt their story, but you are not here to judge their account as their experience is their experience and no one can change that fact. If they feel they saw an alien waving to them from a UFO then no amount of arguing or lack of data will change their perception. Just be sure they understand that critical questioning is crucial to finding the truth behind their experience and is only meant to balance possibilities.

The bottom line so far is to communicate with the client. There should never be any surprises. The more open you are with the client the more they will be open with you as there will be a lot of trust between both parties. Let them know what you will be doing every step of the way and approximately how long it might take.

When you first meet up with the client be sure to be personable. This goes beyond shaking hands and saying hello, be sure to engage in small talk. This will help break the ice, allow them to not be so nervous, and basically show that you are a human being. Take some time initially to get to know them and they will not only respect and trust you, but they will feel more open to be honest and more open about their feelings behind their experience. Be sure to refrain from engaging in conspiracy theory talk or discussion about other aspects related to UFOs. Many clients seem to want to gauge your interest or perceptions about the field before completely opening up, but if they begin to push remind them of what you are there for and that adding your opinions will not provide a focus for their situation.

Once the "small talk" is over and one or both of you want to begin to discuss the event you need to prepare the interviewee. Let them know that first you want to do a small exercise to help them with the interview. Begin by asking them to describe a typical day for them. While they are talking about their average day ask them for clarity and detail, force them to be as descriptive as they can. If they are talking about getting ready for work and are already describing coming home within a minute stop them and go back to the morning. Find one aspect they were very general with and ask specific questions. For example, let's say they state that when they eat breakfast they have eggs, toast, oatmeal, or sometimes cereal and then they go on to the next part of their day. You could stop them and ask them to elaborate more.

"When you described making breakfast, what do you normally eat? How do you prepare these items? Where and how do you eat? Describe what a typical cleanup process of the kitchen following breakfast would be."

Don't ask all of these questions at once, but stagger them as they begin to add information but are still not being descriptive enough. Stop them periodically during their description of their day while allowing about 5 minutes (it's a lot longer than it seems) or more to get through the day. Obviously it's not necessary to go through the whole day, but once they understand that you are forcing them to be more detailed and they begin to do so you can then end this exercise.

This exercise will serve as a warmup to get their mind ready to retrieve the information about their sighting. This also serves to allow you to gain their confidence as well as be able become aware of how they answer questions and is a good warmup for you to start looking at filling in the gaps between information.

When they describe tasks or events of their average day ask how they feel and look for the corresponding emotion on their faces, hands, and other body language that agrees with their statement. Compare their facial expressions and body language to each extreme of emotion and see how they correlate to each other.

This technique is multifaceted; first we are training them to be descriptive, second we are getting a baseline on how they react to questions as well their emotions. As they describe their day be very attentive to how they describe their stressful situations, happy situations, and other emotions in how they use their hands, voice, and overall body language. Third, we are allowing them to relax. The topic of their sighting may be a tense one for them depending upon the case. Obviously we broke the ice earlier, but allowing them to talk about themselves while sitting down during the interview process will typically relax that person a little more which will allow them to concentrate when talking about their personal experience and will ultimately help them to remember more detail.

We talk of baseline readings in equipment prior to conducting a paranormal investigation just as scientists use baseline readings to determine how something works normally. Using the five minute method will help you create a baseline of how the person should react to the same type of emotional context during their description or questions asked of their event. With questioning during the five minute method you can put them into scenarios to push the boundaries of the general emotions (anger, fear, sadness, disgust, contempt, surprise, happiness or joy) to get a feeling for, as well as looking at body language and facial features, at how they react to them. While this isn't absolutely necessary in every case and with all emotions it is worth it to at least see a few of these so you can get a basic feel for how they react emotionally to questions.

If they are describing something and saying they were upset, yet are not displaying the same emotion they may not be telling the truth. If you assume this then you should continue to probe that event from different angles and see if you can match the original context of body language to emotion. It's not a foolproof method and is one that may take some time for some people to master, but it is an additional tool as a researcher and investigator.

In one of my last books, "Handbook for the Amateur Paranormal Investigator: The Art and Science of Paranormal Investigation," I included a chapter on body language basics. In a complex series of events and high emotion it is important to understand how a person is feeling about what they are saying. In an overwhelming majority of UFO cases you will be dealing with a singular event and not ongoing ones. I have kept the subject of body language to a minimum here as to not make it appear as though it is necessary to learn. Merely seeing how a person reacts to situations similar to what they might experience should be enough for most people to understand what is happening with the client.

The favorite subject matter for most people is talking about themselves. This isn't a bad thing and it will definitely give you a good look at how they express themselves as their "guard" will be down since they should be relaxed. If you warned them in the beginning that some of the questions might be tough, be sure to reaffirm this fact during this point as you should push a few boundaries to find out about the emotions I listed, no matter how simple the case. Remind them that what you are doing is necessary to help gather information about their incident and that you will explain everything in time. If you divulge what you are doing, about reading their body language, you will make them think about what they are doing which will be completely counterproductive for this approach. You have to be as natural as possible if you use this method and it should be the only time you come close to deceiving a client.

A specific method for extracting more information is outlined below and is used in police and other law enforcement agencies all over the world. This technique is called the cognitive interview. It is a series of steps, that when used correctly, will get the client to remember more detail then just asking them to explain what happened (Geiselman and Fisher).

This process will be much longer than a standard interview or having them merely tell you a story or filling out a questionnaire. However, you will get much more detailed information and will be able to gauge their emotions.

The cognitive interview approach is broken into four distinct sections that should be used in this order for it to be effective. There are a couple of variations of the cognitive interview, but I have found this to be the most common and easiest for amateur interviewers to perform.

1. **Reconstruct the circumstances**. Have the witness start with what they were doing before the event occurred. Have them describe their mood and the setting of the location of the event. The witness should be able to describe as much as possible about their self (what they were thinking, feeling, etc.) and the environment prior to the event occurring. This information is two-fold. First, it will help them remember more detail about what took place. Second, it will give us possible clues as to the possibility of logical explanations.

2.   **Report everything**. A client may hold back information because they may not think it is important to the overall case. Telling them to not hold anything back is important to help their memory in telling the story. This is the point in which you would have them tell their story. As the witness is telling their story be sure to think of and write down questions. First allow them to tell their story uninterrupted. Once they are done go back and ask questions to help fill in the gaps starting from prior to the sighting to during and then after. Ask them specific information about the setting during the story; location of pets, were the lights on inside or out, did they notice anything else happening outside, etc. Also, with each change in context be sure to get specifics about their feelings along the way. Using the present tense you might ask, "What do you see?" or "How do you feel about what you see?" This encourages more detail through remembering. As you go through the story these detailed questions will help jog their memory and by giving their feelings they are more likely to connect to the event to remember even more about it.

3.   **Recall the events in a different order**. When the witness has completed their story and you have asked your initial set of detailed questions tell them you want them to tell the story backwards or from various points forward. This isn't to thwart a liar, but to go back and break up parts of the event and dig deeper into it. You might ask, "What is going on before you saw the UFO fly over the yard?" You might add "Describe everything about the scene" or "Of what you have told me, what stands out?" Go on to the next scene, if applicable, and repeat the process. This will allow the witness' brain to really begin to remember fine details about the event.

4.   **Change perspective**. Have the witness attempt to recall the events from another perspective. This could be from the viewpoint of another person in the room at the time or from

a different location relevant to the event such as a rock or tree that offers perspective to the sighting. This will allow you to continue to ask a variety of questions looking for details and emotions about what they perceived about the event.

Cognitive interviewing allows the interviewer the ability to access the memory of the witness by several different methods. Our memory has several different access points and exploring these various approaches within this interview allows us to explore many options and allow us to access details in ways that may be stronger in one person than another.

It's a technique that takes some getting used to, especially if you are not comfortable with interviewing people. Again, communication with the client is important and if you explain you are going to be asking them a series of questions, be sure to explain things as you go.

During the process be sure to ask questions at every step of the way. When asking questions be sure to use open ended questions and avoid closed ended ones. Instead of asking "How did seeing the UFO make you feel?" ask "What was going through your mind as you saw the UFO?" The first question will typically generate a one word response; scared, nervous, frightened, etc. Allowing them to tap into their emotions instead of merely tagging it with an easy or expected emotion you can get more information behind the sighting. With the second question you can use their answer to ask more open ended questions to further probe details about what they saw or how they felt.

Also, avoid using leading questions. In other words, instead of asking "Did seeing the UFO scare you?" again ask what they were thinking or feeling at the time. A leading question gives them an expected emotion and a free answer. The key here is for them to tap into their experience and answer from the heart and their true memory.

Before or after the cognitive interview it is helpful to find out where they get their perception of the event. Have they read books or seen a recent television show or news item on a similar subject? How did they feel about the subject prior to having their experience? How do they feel about it now? This information can help you identify a potential bias toward specific events or thoughts. If a person just watched *Independence Day* on television then their perception of the environment might be geared toward being a bit nervous about UFOs or have them on the brain instead of a potential logical explanation for what they saw.

The final step of the interview process is to have them fill out a form detailing their particular sighting. You may have used one during a follow up phone call or used one to jot down information as you questioned them, but provide them with a clean one to write out further information about their sighting. Let them take it home and then collect it when they are finished or provide them a self-addressed stamped envelope or mailer to send it back to you in a timely manner. Having it paid for in advance will encourage the witness to send it back to you. I find that it is easier to merely ask them the questions and fill out the form yourself as it will cut out the wait time for getting it completed.

When interviewing the client feel free to take notes, but do not let the notes slow down the interview. Allowing the client to talk non-stop is essential and paying attention to them is essential for two way communication. This is another key to recording the conversation. You may also record the interview on video, but never do so in a public setting such as a restaurant and always let the client know that you will be doing this prior to meeting for the interview.

If it is essential to write something down just use short groups of words or wait until the client is done with their thought and then ask for the information again. Hopefully you are able to record the interview so your note taking will be at a minimum. This is also where using a second person can come in handy.

If using a second person you can be free to ask questions while your partner writes down the answers. This will allow you to watch the witness for body language cues and acknowledge them during the conversation (nodding in agreement, maintaining eye contact, etc.) which will encourage them to share more information. You will also have the ability to write down questions that appear outside of the form that the other interviewer can be following. This will allow for more information to be documented.

If a digital recorder is used this will also free you up to pay attention to the client. Just be careful not to rely on the recorder for all of the information gathered, technology isn't always fool proof and just in case it dies or the memory becomes full during the interview or the audio isn't good enough to disseminate. The other problem is listening to the interview again and stopping constantly to take notes. I will usually take notes during an interview and listen to the audio later while reviewing what I wrote. This way I can follow along and make additional comments or thoughts along with what I wrote.

If using a second interviewer it will be good to ask them their opinion once the interview is over and you are away from the client (but not while you are driving). Even if the person has no interest in the sighting they should be able to give an opinion to the story as well as add their thoughts to what was said. In some cases, such as a current sighting, you won't have much time to disseminate the interview as fieldwork will be a step that is needed as soon as possible.

Remind the client that you will communicate with them at every step of the investigation and that it may take time to gather some information. Also request that they keep in touch with you as well if they decide to contact others (state or government resources, media, or other groups) so that you are aware of others involved or if the story will be in the newspaper the next day. Remind them that all of their information will be kept private and nothing will be shared especially prior to any findings are made conclusive.

Chapter 4: Onsite Investigation

The client has been interviewed and you have their statement and other information in regards to their sighting. The UFO may not have crashed or landed in the client's backyard, but there are still many things to do at the site before heading home. In this chapter we will discuss some basic methods of looking for evidence in certain circumstances at the scene of the sighting, obviously every case will be different and there are a number of things you should consider prior to spending your time looking for evidence.

A UFO sighting might seem as though it is just 100% witness testimony and that we just have to take their word for it and sit around and hope for other reports to turn up. There are many things we need to do at the scene of the sighting in order to help corroborate the story as well as potentially provide a logical solution for what the person(s) observed.

One thing to avoid here is using the scene of the sighting for the interview. While it might be enticing to bring the witness to the scene to put both together it will more than likely be counterproductive. In order to truly understand what the witness saw you must rely on their ability to remember what they saw without distractions. Being at the scene is a major distraction and may cause them to remember the sighting a different way or to add things that did not happen while they are observing the location. Being at the scene is not conducive to the cognitive interview as you need the witness to rely on memory not the physical scene. Once you get their testimony then take them to the scene. Once there be on the lookout to see if they begin adding details and other information.

Before searching for evidence of a UFO we have to again be careful not to jump to conclusions. A witness might say the UFO hit the tops of the trees and the evidence are dozens of broken pieces of wood in the backyard. Before scooping up all of these pieces we might want to look at the historical weather for that area to see if a storm has gone through the area recently. The easiest resource for this is Weather Underground at https://www.wunderground.com/. Once you enter the zip code from the area you can click a link to "History" and change the date.

Is it necessary to put all of these tree branches in bags and send them off to be analyzed for UFO paint for a hit and run? Probably not. The only evidence you need to take for analysis is anything that has been altered by a potential UFO contact. Yes, a branch has been altered but a number of things could be responsible and if we cannot see where a collision took place we would really have nothing to gain by collecting pieces.

If there was a landing or anything looks suspicious enough to collect or create casts for be sure to photograph it from every angle before touching it. Close ups, far away, ground level, eye level, using a measuring tape for scale, as well as including a potential pathway of movement should be documented in photos before doing anything.

The major piece of the onsite investigation is verifying some of the information of the scene from the witness. It's not as if we don't trust the witness, but we just need to visually and physically verify certain parts of the scene for our upcoming research.

For these observations you will obviously have to be at the original scene of the sighting. Have the client stand or sit in the same exact position as when they first saw the object and walk you through their entire sighting as you observe. If they were in a car or on a bicycle it is important to be able to reenact this as closely as possible. Obviously if they were driving down a freeway in the speed lane we would not want to park the car in that spot, but we could drive down that location to get a feel for it or pull off the side of the road safely near the same spot to be able to see and document the location.

Once they are done describing their sighting you can then verify the direction in which the object was first seen through where it was last seen. You can use a compass or a variety of smart phone based apps to help you determine the direction (north, east, south, or west) of the location of the object from the observer. Smart phone applications can also provide a plethora of other information including latitude and longitude, azimuth and bearing, and the app named Dioptra can take a photograph of a scene with all of this information in the background along with time and date for future reference.

Taking photographs as reference is also something that should be done. A photo of where the client was looking when the first saw the event followed by subsequent shots of the movement of the craft should be taken. It is also suggested to take photographs to show what is behind where the person was standing or in the case of being inside of a car or building document the inside with photographs (especially with dashboard and radio lights on if the event happened at night). When taking photographs for documentation you will want to write down what each photograph is. Do not rely on your memory later on to tell you what is in the photograph or where it is pointed. Without documentation and knowing what these photos are of exactly they are pretty much useless. Do not photograph the witness without their consent!

Also from the vantage point of the witness we can determine an estimated distance. If we are standing along a road and the object went behind one tree but not another object we can then determine the distance. It probably won't be this easy as most objects are merely seen in the sky and will not have such details to paint an accurate picture of distance. Without an accurate distance it will be difficult to verify elevation and speed as well.

Determining direction is one of the things we should be able to figure out with just working with the witness and the scene. The object went left to right and seemed to fade away as it went. This description allows us to understand the direction that the UFO took when passing through the area where the witness saw it.

If the object might fit the description of a Chinese lantern this is the clue you need to pursue this evidence. This is where using a map such as Google Earth can come in handy. From this vantage point we can mark an imaginary line that marks the area over which the UFO might have traveled. If we start from before where the object was seen and trace it backward and start from where the object was last seen and trace forward we might be able to find traces of a Chinese lantern in the trees, power lines, or even on the ground. It might seem pointless to search, but again, we have to look at all possible explanations and if the sighting seems to fit a low hanging slowly moving UFO with a dull yellow to orange light we should accept the possibility that it could be a Chinese lantern and investigate as thoroughly as we can for that possibility. Even if we do not find evidence we cannot assume that the lantern was not a possibility.

If a client claims that a UFO landed or created damage to their property you might need to bring equipment that can detect radiation. This equipment (radiation detector, Geiger counter, or dosimeter) can be rented or even bought online. A Kearny Fallout Meter, which is a basic radiation detector, can even be built at home (http://readynutrition.com/resources/a-step-by-step-guide-for-how-to-make-a-kearny-fallout-meter_08082012/).

Other equipment used on scene might include binoculars, a magnifying glass, compass, measuring tape, flashlights, large plastic bags, markers to mark them, camera, and a pen and pad to write down observations as well as photographs taken at the scene. You can never document any type of investigation too much. It is highly recommended that you carry as much of these items as possible in your vehicle or in a bag ready to head out to an investigation.

When searching property for evidence you will want to begin by taking documentation photographs at a distance. The second step would be to draw out a basic map of the property and divide it into sections based on markers seen on the property. The sections should be divided out into even squares so that they can be broken

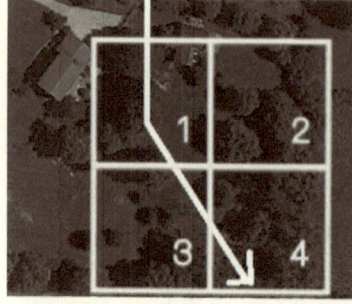

down further and any evidence can be marked on the map. When searching for evidence of any kind begin in one square and search thoroughly before moving to another section. In the accompanying photo the house is just to the left of the squares and the backyard is broken into four

quadrants. The path of the UFO as seen from the home took a turn as they thought that it had hit the large tree in their backyard.

There are a variety of ways of searching for evidence, but grid and spiral searches will probably be your best bet in most areas. For

a grid search you will want to start alone one of the boundary lines and walk along it to the far side. You will then turn and head back into the same quadrant only a few inches or feet away from the outside boundary line. As you hit the end on the same line you began you will then go the same distance away going back and forth until you reach

the end of the boundary. From there you will repeat this pattern heading in the other two directions back and forth. For example, if

you went north, south, north, south, etc. first you would then go east and west tracing the same pattern.

The spiral search pattern is just what it sounds like. Starting in the center of the quadrant you would walk in a circle slowly moving to the

outside of the area. You would try hard to keep the movement in a circle uniform while keeping an eye to the ground for any type of clue that might need collected for testing. A good way to assist with this is to drive a stake in the ground in the middle of the search area. Tie thin string to the stake and use it as a tether to ensure that you are slowly walking from the center as you round the center area. This method works best in a large area devoid of obstacles such as trees.

As mentioned already, any evidence that is suspected to be caused or a piece of potential UFO parts should be photographed close up (with a measuring tape next to for context), from near, as well as from a distance showing part of the backdrop in which it was found while still being able to see the object in the photo before touching it. Try to take as many photographs as possible of the scene as it may come in handy later on during research.

The physical collection process of any potential evidence should also be photographed. No object should be physically touched and gloves or other clean instruments should be used to collect objects and placed into bags. The bags should be marked as to where the evidence was found, who collected it, as well as the time and date it was collected. Any gloves or objects used to collect the object should also be bagged separately and labeled just in case there was potential contamination.

Physical evidence only exists if the UFO has made some sort of change to the environment. Branches may fall all the time, but if it collided with the tree the branches may have other marks on them or potentially other materials noticeably rubbed off on them. If a UFO landed there may be scorch marks or deep impressions in the grass.

One area that people tend to get excited about is circles of discolored grass. Many people feel that these discolorations mean that a UFO has landed in their yard. An overwhelming majority of these are referred to as fairy rings that are steeped in folklore that are said to have fairies that can abduct you and take you to other lands (Basterfield). While you more than likely will not get abducted by fairies or aliens it helps to understand that these discolored rings are actually caused by fungi (Dicklow) and are quite common all over the world.

The analysis of samples should happen as soon as possible after collecting them. You will probably not have the ability or access to analyze samples for trace evidence and will more than likely have to send them out for testing. I would highly recommend that even if you do have the ability or access that you still send out partial samples for independent analysis.

Plant or soil samples should be sent to an agricultural university after contacting someone at the facility to find out if testing can be done. Geologists, biologists, chemists, and even engineers might need to be referred to when attempting to determine the origin or impact on the environment of evidence. Never ship anything that you suspect is radioactive as this would be more than just frowned upon by the USPS.

Granted, most UFO cases will not enjoy the potential success of leftover clues. The majority of time spent at the scene should be on observation. Do you see or hear airplanes moving through the sky? Are there contrails left from high flying jets? Are there other potential explanations that exist toward the line of sight of the viewer?

There could be a car dealership or other business a mile or so away that had been using a searchlight for a promotion on the night the witness saw the UFO. This information might come from researching the area after the fact, but if you can determine that a business is in the line of sight you may want to visit to ask. This might also include fireworks displays from fairs or other times away from the 4th of July. This might be part of research, but can also be answered quickly by merely asking those that are in the area other than the witness.

Observation of the area should also include the surrounding area away from the location and especially in the direction of where the UFO was seen coming and going. It is possible that someone owns a drone in this area or a remote control aircraft club practices close to the area that might not be known any other way except by walking or driving around the area observing.

Observation can also include nighttime observation if the sighting was fairly recent. This isn't to say that you expect a repeat performance of a UFO zooming overheard, but it can help to spot potential explanations and document, record, or directly show the witness. While it would be helpful to be in the same exact location where the witness saw their UFO it might also be of help to view the same sky from another angle. This will work well especially if you cannot get permission to be at the home of the witness or if the area is inaccessible such as a freeway.

If conducting a nighttime observation you will want to be on the lookout for airplane routes mostly around the time the UFO report was made. Smaller commercial or private craft may take unfamiliar flight paths near homes that might catch the homeowner off-guard.

Chapter 5: Offsite Research

Offsite research might not sound as sexy as the onsite investigation but it is just as important and can cover many other types of UFO reports. This research allows you to take the information gathered at the site and look for other potential logical answers to what the witness might have seen as well as look for other cases in the area that may offer more information as well.

Offsite research is not just for looking up information via Google for an ongoing case but also includes looking at evidence sent to you for analysis such as photographs, videos, or stories that someone believes to be true (come one, we know everything is true on the Internet).

The offsite research from a case you have begun to investigate might include a closer look at Google Earth. Looking up mapping software on your phone may not give you an ample look at the entire surroundings of the location of where a witness described seeing a UFO. Being able to sit down and look at a large screen with minimal distractions will give you the chance to look for information that you may have overlooked from talking to the witness and canvassing the area.

You might have known where the local municipal and regional airports were, but viewing them on a map gives you a better idea if it is possible that an airplane from one of these airports might have been the UFO the witness saw. Having some time to really dig into a map can give you a much better perspective on the area than just driving around and would be a great idea to do if you plan on go on a night observation of the area.

Looking at an overhead map will also give you a different perspective to the overall scene that you just investigated and along with the photographs of the scene you can get a better sense of where the UFO might have been in relation to the viewer and surrounding area. You may even want to look at topographical maps to view elevation changes in the land as an additional guide, but Google Earth does a good job at simulating this and is much better than just using Google Maps.

Another advantage with Google Earth over Google Maps is the ability to draw a line and measure distance right on the map. The ring menu has selections like file, edit, view, tools, and more. Clicking on tools it will have a dropdown menu that you can then check ruler. The ruler will pop up on the map and will start where you click on the map and will stay attached to one end of the ruler until you click again. It might take some getting used to as you can zoom in and out using the scroll button on a mouse and use the left click to drag your way across the map. When you merely click with the left button the ruler will end and you will have a measurement from one area to another.

Other mapping you software that I highly recommend is Stellarium (http://www.stellarium.org/). Stellarium is a free open sourced planetarium software that allows you to look at the sky from anywhere at any time. Obviously the sky is simulated and not live, but you have the ability to go back in time to a particular time and place and look in a direction to see what the witness would have seen in the sky of explained stars and planets. The software may take a bit of time to get used to so I would recommend downloading it and playing around with it. The majority of the controls are located along the bottom and on the lower left edge. Along the left you will be able to change the day, time, location, and many other aspects in order to view the sky at the time the witness would have seen it.

One website that accompanies planetarium software would be ones that track large satellites including the International Space Station (ISS). As previously mentioned, the website Heavens Above (http://www.heavens-above.com/) allows you to look at historical information of the sky by plugging in an exact location and adjusting it on a map. From there you can click on a particular satellite, or predictions for the brightest satellites, or even for predicted iridium flares which are the reflections of the sun from satellites during evening or morning hours when the sun is set but still able to be reflected at high altitudes.

There are other satellite tracking websites some of which I have already mentioned and have included at the end of this book in the resources section under Chapter 4: Further Information. Another key is to attempt to back up any findings you may think you have against another resource if possible, especially in regards to satellites or astronomical data. One website might seem like great work on your part to say that Sirius was in the same spot the witness observed a bright light that seemed to follow him, but two sites stating the same thing is a slam dunk.

Research may also include the dissemination of photographs or video taken at the scene or ones that the witness claims they did not see while filming. For many, a photograph is the proof they have of their encounter and many times it helps in providing a logical solution and other times the photograph merely makes things more confusing. The goal is to balance the information if necessary and focus on the aspect (statement or evidence) that can help explain what happened to the witness.

Photographs have always been a question mark in science. In 2015 a rare hummingbird was photographed during an expedition in Columbia in South America. The blue-bearded helmetcrest had not been seen since 1946 and scientists felt that the bird had become extinct due to excessive habitat loss (Casey). However, this single photograph verified the existence of this once thought extinct species.

Another bird, the Jerdon's babbler, was rediscovered and photographed in Myanmar after not being seen in over 70 years. A series of photographs helped prove that this bird still existed. The use of digital photography to validate birds is a hotly debated topic, just as it is viewed as proof of ghosts, cryptids, or UFOs. Can one photograph prove the existence of UFOs?

As mentioned earlier, UFO photos and videos are many times used to serve as centerpieces in hoaxes. You should always have your guard up when receiving photographs or videos as potential evidence especially if there is not much more the witness can add other than what is seen in the video or if the story and photograph don't seem to match up. You should also have at least a decent idea of what to look for when analyzing photographs and videos to be on the lookout for not only logical solutions but potential hoaxes through digital manipulation.

There are entire websites and YouTube channels that operate on nothing more than UFO photographs and videos. Luckily, there are also websites that exist for nothing more than finding logical solutions for or exposing hoaxes of UFO photographs and videos. My favorite rational website on UFO evidence is https://www.ufoofinterest.org/ which needs to be translated to English as a website, but you can also follow him along on Twitter @ufoofinterest.

A viewer may see an everyday object, but misperceive it due to strange circumstances such as an airplane flying into or away from

the setting sun creating a bright reflection and appearing as a strange object flying away (seen in upper left of photo courtesy of Metabunk.org). Other objects might be either misinterpreted from the distance from it or intentionally taken out of context such as the upper right and two lower photographs seen here (courtesy UFO of Interest) that are just an out of focus jet at high altitude.

Factor in other things such as lens flares and long exposure not to mention all of the digital manipulation programs such as Adobe and canvas painters such as CinePaint and you have a recipe for deception than even a 14 year old kid can bake. I could probably write an entire book just about the types of misinterpretations of objects or photography as well as how to decode them, but I will offer the basic information on the subject.

A client will more than likely present a photograph as evidence over a video, but as cell phone cameras begin to have more space and better lenses the media type might be an even race. The most important thing is to understand the context and location that the photograph was taken in. A photograph might show a wonderfully detailed UFO in a picturesque location, but once revealed to be taken from a bed and breakfast or rental location kitchen and the UFO is more than likely a reflection from inside.

The photograph in this paragraph took Facebook by storm in August of 2015 (pun intended). The photo was shared with the description, "This photo was taken in Australia, get it out there as Facebook are trying to remove it." And people shared it, over 700,000 people shared it. Meanwhile, the original photograph was traced by to an imgur account and was posted on July 18, 2015, with the headline, "The reflection of the light inside makes it look like there's a UFO." The image  was actually taken at the Signal Mountain Lodge in Wyoming. To date, this photograph has over 1.8 million views from the original imgur site and millions more from UFO believers.

Many UFO photographs are taken from inside vehicles which pose a couple of major issues. The first issue is that the person is driving or even as a passenger it is hard to not only see but to interpret what one is seeing. Many UFO photographs are taken through the windshield. A bug, smudge, chip, or anything else on the windshield might become blurry in the photograph and with the background become larger in appearance than it actually is. This has explained one of my favorite ghost videos as well as the camera panned as the car took a turn and it appeared that a misty ghost walked across the road. In reality, the camera panned across the smudge mark on the windshield fighting what to focus on making it appear as though the ghost was moving across the road.

In the photograph in this paragraph the still shot was taken from a video titled, "Chasing a Huge UFO Mother Ship". The video begins at the stop light and just before the car moves forward when the light turns green the shot is panned back which gives the illusion that the "ship", or rather chip, is moving away from the car as it pursues it. What we are actually seeing is a chip in the windshield that is  conveniently centered in the camera. This video was more than likely posted innocently, but the pullback effect seems to have been done during filming and more than likely not done after the fact so it might have been meant to be misleading or just for fun.

Another issue with cars falls very much in line with the prior example of the lodge. Many people present photographs taken within vehicles at night. This obviously presents another series of potential issues with reflected light. In many photographs a UFO is nothing more than a lens flare from a street or parking lot lamp. These "UFOs" are created by the bright light creating an artifact in the image. A lens flare can happen during the day or during the  night as long as there is a bright enough object such as the sun or a street light.

In January of 2008, Karolina-Slavka Mueller, a student visiting London took three photographs from within a vehicle that showed what was described as a "classic flying saucer". The photographs circulated the Internet and experts were baffled. This had to be a real event since the same

UFO was in three different photographs, right?

UFO researcher, cameraman, and editor Chris Martin was quoted by the online newspaper *The Sun* as saying, "I was looking for evidence that these have been fabricated…..I couldn't find any evidence. It's unprecedented because she produced three pictures, which seems to show it's flying…..My own evaluation is that these photographs are genuine and have not been digitally manipulated or hoaxed…..These photos are, in my opinion as a UFO researcher, absolutely astounding and show a real object seemingly under intelligent control." The photograph more than likely was not digitally manipulated, but the UFO in question is highly likely the interior reflection of one of the gauges that was backlit on the dashboard cluster. Many UFO "experts" were fooled by this for months (Naisbitt).

The three examples I have shown of UFO photographs might seem silly, but when they came out they fooled a lot of people. When first seeing most of these examples many people had a hard time figuring them out, but once the pieces come together and the mystery is lifted for a solid logical explanation it is easy to see the illusion.

Again, many times a person will claim they did not see a UFO when they took a picture. These are very hard to accept as potential evidence since the location is a question mark. If we can go to that location and the photograph was taken recently we might be able to replicate the photograph or see what might have caused it. If not and a viable solution cannot be presented the photograph should be deemed "inconclusive". This is not to say that it is unexplainable, but that a solution was not easily discovered, but the photograph was taken with questionable means.

Even if a witness watches a UFO flying through the sky and photographs it we still have to be skeptical even if an explanation is not readily available. Photographs serve as documentation and not as proof of anything. If a witness sees a UFO and photographs or video tapes it the evidence does not qualify it as proof of a UFO encounter, it merely acts as validation of their experience. In the example of a bird being validated by photographs they have been collected and studied in the past so a photograph merely documents what is already proven to exist.

When I first started out as a ghost investigator we took photos with 35MM cameras. This meant we could only take 24 or 36 photos with a roll of film and then we would have to drop it off for an hour or a couple of days to see what we took. With digital technology we can instantly see what the camera saw and review how well it represents what we see and if any adjustments need made.

One of the most important facets of photo research is getting the original file sent to you. In the early days this meant asking a client to borrow their original negatives used to create their pictures. With digital technology it is simply copying and sharing the original file that was on the file holding format for that camera at the time. This might mean forwarding a picture from a cell phone or file from a SD card which is much simpler than snail mailing someone their negatives back.

Once you get a photograph, and if it is a case you are working, first compare it to the location in which the client stated they saw the UFO. You should have reference photographs of the location and scene of the sighting (as well as various angles) as a resource. Does the weather match the witness statement? Is it the right time of the year? You did remember to take reference photographs of the scene, right?

If the photograph is merely sent to you one of the first things you want to do after looking at it is use a Google image search or upload the photograph to Tineye. These two sources are great for finding photographs that are already available online. However, if a photo is cropped or tampered with it may not appear in these programs.

In just one of dozens of examples I have researched over the years this photo accompanied a long drawn out story about the government creation of top secret space craft based on Nazi technology. The photo, along with an ever-changing storyline, wandered around the Internet until the real photograph was located and the story was essentially debunked since the photo was the main part of the story.

The reality was the photograph was used in a short fictional movie created by Seb Janiak called "The Orion Conspiracy". It was essentially a fictional 20 minute top secret meeting where a man read the history of the coverup of UFO knowledge by the U.S. and other governments (you can find it on YouTube and at the

reference at the end of this paragraph). Janiak is a French photographer and director who created many of the slides used in the film and used many others which were known fakes (Koi).

The photograph is of an F-14B Tomcat jet fighter that was taken during a salvage operation in Crete. The original photograph was uploaded to Flickr. This particular fighter jet was lost in the Mediterranean Sea during carrier launch operations in 2002. The aircraft was recovered in June of 2002 in nearly 10,000

feet of water which I think is just as incredible even if it wasn't an enhanced photo of a fake UFO. A fake propulsion system was added to the bottom of the jet and a guy in a black suit was dropped to supervise for good measure.

Your next step should be viewing the metadata or EXIF information included on the file of the photograph. This can help you identify when, potentially where and especially how the photograph was taken. The settings will help tell you a story as to the type of camera, lighting conditions and if the flash was used, as well as a lot of other information that should be considered to help understand the conditions in which the photo was taken. One great program for reviewing this information and looking for altered files is JPEGsnoop (https://sourceforge.net/projects/jpegsnoop/).

You can also find websites that can identify EXIF data within photographs that are found online. FindEXIF.com is a great resource where you can paste the URL of a photograph online to see the EXIF information. Just simply right click on any photograph and click on "Copy image address" and go to the box to enter the information and right click again to paste. Foto Forensics in another wonder program (http://fotoforensics.com/) which you can use a URL or upload a photograph to get EXIF information and can help you identify if portions were digitally manipulated after the photo was taken.

Some easy telltales about the validity of photographs include pixelization. If the photo is blurry in one spot or seems pixelated in a particular area where a UFO is or where other objects might have been inserted this may point to a potentially altered photograph. Also when analyzing a photograph take time to get an understanding of where the light sources are in the photograph. If there are shadows (or lack thereof) that are in the wrong place this may signal digital manipulation. Shadows can sometimes be misleading, but in some cases a few misplaced shadows was enough to debunk a picture that would have been impossible to tell otherwise. Shadows and reflections can be measured to see if they are in a straight line from the sources, if not you have a fake on your hands.

Another simple trick of quick evaluation is focus. If an object is close to the camera and is in focus an object far away should not be. Objects that display the same focus should be at about the same distance from the lens under basic or automatic settings.

If you are going to analyze photographs I would highly recommend that you learn about cameras and how certain issues happen within them. Lens flares and slow shutter speed are two of the main culprits behind anomalous photographs that are not tampered with. Understanding how issues are created in photographs as well as how the settings affect this is critical if you desire to tear apart this data.

I had wanted to create a chapter just for photo and video research, but decided that the scope of this book is for the amateur or average researcher. While I love to take photographs and have an above average knowledge of camera operations and issues I ultimately felt that this book should stay as a foundation of knowledge and not a complete resource for any of the information covered. I don't want you, the reader, to rely on this book for all of your knowledge as this book is merely a stepping stone.

Video analysis is a little tougher. Even ten years ago it was very easy to spot a manipulated video or photograph. As mentioned already even a young teenager can create a video that would rival movies made about a decade ago in Hollywood. Analyzing these also means researching the stories behind them as well as the extra information seen in the video that can tell you more about what, when, where, and why the video was shot.

A dead giveaway to a fake UFO video is when the shot is seemingly set up just for this event. While people are very creative in making fake anomalous videos they are seemingly more focused on creating a great CGI effect rather than truly convincing the viewer that the person filming was actually seeing a UFO. Many of these videos have a camera that is seemingly shooting a random spot in the sky and the UFO is almost obviously put into the scene and the whole video just doesn't feel right. We would not expect someone to film a UFO with precision and be able to follow the every move of it. Although it is easy to get caught up in the "human nature" side of the argument we should always evaluate the facts that we see within the video as well as any statements made about the sighting. In the end there are always details that don't match up or make sense and this can easily debunk a video.

One highly overlooked area of videos is sound. One UFO video I saw had what sounded like dozens of people shouting yet the shouts did not match what the scene was nor did I see anyone in the video actually shouting or even seemingly appearing concerned about anything but being filmed. Some videos put UFO sounds in them flying away or flying across the sky. Simple science would say that the sound will change as an object moves away or past the viewer and it should not stay the same. Physics has to apply to UFOs no matter where they are, but especially here on Earth!

Ultimately, we should honestly view UFO photographs and videos for what they most likely are; misinterpretations and assumptions. These pieces of evidence serve to enhance the person's experience if they are part of what the witness has seen. If the images were taken without a visual experience they are merely circumstantial and could be anything from bugs to CGI and it is honestly not worth your time to analyze images and video where the witness did not directly observe what occurred in the photograph or video.

The real reason for this is that UFOs have never been proven to exist and we should be very doubtful about this simplistic evidence since there are so many easy explanations as well as ways to misinterpret and manipulate them. Videos sent to you where the person feels strongly that it is a UFO you will find that they will more than likely not accept your findings anyway. So, no, one photograph cannot prove UFOs exist and we as a culture of UFO researchers and investigators need to stop assuming this is the case.

To wrap up this chapter, the offsite research of an ongoing witness case should include everything you can imagine to look for potential logical explanations such as the ones highlighted in chapter 2 of part 2 of this book. The witness statement will serve as a guide as to what the person might have seen and the details may help you lean toward one specific type, but it is your research that will lead the way in finding out if any one or more explanations can logically account for what the witness saw or what they documented in photos or video.

The key is to allow the evidence to speak for the case and to not make assumptions. Again, this not only goes for jumping to the conclusion that this was definitely an alien powered spacecraft or a secret government test vehicle but for trying to merely explain it away. Unfortunately, an overwhelming majority of UFO cases are explainable.

The Project Blue Book Special Report #14 was an attempt to statistically classify the more than 3,200 cases collected by the U.S. Air Force from 1947 to 1952. The report declared that 69% of the cases were explainable with 38% of the explainable cases being conclusively identified while 31% of explainable cases were "doubtfully" explained. The report also showed that 9% of total cases contained insufficient data. The remaining 22% of cases were deemed to be unexplained (U.S. Air Force). This isn't to say that these cases were UFOs flown by aliens, but that they did not have a sufficient answer one way or the other to make a determination.

What's more interesting is that Project Blue Book continued to collect cases until 1970 and the number of unidentified cases dropped dramatically. At the end of its run the number of unidentified cases was only at 6% (Wikipedia contributors).

Many other studies and collections of UFO reports show varying numbers of reports that remain unidentified with most of them below 10%. Even those that remain unexplained may have some sort of logical outcome that was never discovered or validated. Of the identified reports of varying reporting agencies and studies it should be pointed out that astronomical and aircraft explanations accounted for well more than half of all of the reports. This historical point should be enough to put your work into perspective; odds are very good that the case you are exploring will have a logical outcome if you look for the right things. Your goal is to exhaust everything you can think of to explain it before labeling it unexplained.

Part IV: Resources

Chapter 1: Encounter Classifications

Josef Allen Hynek was an astronomer, professor, and author with a Ph.D. in astrophysics which he completed at Yerkes Observatory in Wisconsin. Hynek was hired by the U.S. government as a consultant for Project Sign (1947-1949) where was very skeptical of reports. He assisted the U.S. Air Force through Project Grudge (1949-1952), and finally with Project Blue Book (1952-1969). These attempts first began to look at whether the sightings were of any real scientific value and eventually morphed into whether they posed any national security threat.

Hynek felt that these attempts were set up to fail and that those who seemed to have a bit of belief were not kept with the programs as they moved forward. This complete debunk of the concept annoyed him and at the same time he began to gather data that made him question his stance of hardcore skepticism. In a 1985 interview with Dennis Stacy where he was asked what changed his perception of the UFO phenomenon where he said,

"Two things, really. One was the completely negative and unyielding attitude of the Air Force. They wouldn't give UFOs the chance of existing, even if they were flying up and down the street in broad daylight. Everything had to have an explanation. I began to resent that, even though I basically felt the same way, because I still thought they weren't going about it in the right way. You can't assume that everything is black no matter what. Secondly, the caliber of the witnesses began to trouble me. Quite a few instances were reported by military pilots, for example, and I knew them to be fairly well-trained, so this is when I first began to think that, well, maybe there something to all this." (Stacy).

Hynek is considered the "father" of the scientific investigation of UFOs. He created the Center for UFO Studies in 1973 (CUFOS). In his first book, *The UFO Experience: A Scientific Inquiry*, Hynek wrote about the close encounters scale. His scale introduced the three kinds of encounters although others would later add variations to these.

Hynek's scale is broken into two sets of three observations. The first set is for distant sightings and the second are for close encounters. Distant, in regards to this classification, means no closer than 500 feet. Close encounters would then only occur within 500 feet. This was to keep the confusion over what the witness was seeing to a complete minimum to insure they did not mistake a UFO for a known craft.

Hynek Classification System:

Distant

- **(NL)** Nocturnal Lights- Lights seen in the night sky that cannot be explained by natural phenomena.

- **(DD)** Daylight Disc – Any object (regardless of actual shape) that cannot be explained as convention aircraft or other known object.

- **(R/V)** Radar/Visual – These are objects that are seen visually (either by pilots or grounded observers) with the object appearing on radar simultaneously.

Close Encounters

- **(CE1)** Close Encounters of the First Kind – An unknown object seen within 500 feet at detail which does not interact with the physical environment.

- **(CE2)** Close Encounters of the Second Kind – An unknown object within 500 feet that has an effect on the environment or of living organisms. (Examples include; landing gear on the ground flattening grass/soil, vegetation damage, chemical residue, electronics being shut off, people experiencing radiation burns, paralysis, dizziness, or pets reacting, and so on.)

- **(CE3)** Close Encounters of the Third Kind – A figure, perceived pilot, or other type of occupant (robot, humanoid, typical "alien", or other), is viewed within or outside of the craft within 500 feet of the observer.

  Ted Bloecher, who worked with NICAP and CUFOS, suggested further classifications to Hynek's CE3 classification:

  - **A** – Entity is only seen within the craft.
  - **B** – Entity is seen inside and outside the craft.
  - **C** – Entity is seen near the craft, but not observed going in or out.
  - **D** – Entity is observed independently of a craft. A craft sighting has possibly been seen in the area, but not by this specific observer.
  - **E** – Entity is observed, but no UFO is seen by the observer or no sighting is reported in the area at the time the entity is observed.
  - **F**- No entities or UFOs are observed by the witness, but they are contacted by extra sensory perception or other intelligent means.

Other additions to the original system:

- **(CE4)** Close Encounters of the Fourth Kind – Where a person feels they have been abducted by a craft and/or its occupants.

- **(CE5)** Close Encounters of the Fifth Kind – An event where there is direct communication between humans and aliens or occupants of a UFO.

- **(CE6)** Close Encounters of the Sixth Kind – A UFO sighting that leads to the death of a human or animal. Some suggest this might be an extension of the CE2 or at least a severe consequence.

- **(CE7)** Close Encounters of the Seventh Kind – A human/alien hybrid created by regular intercourse or through various other methods.

Jacques Vallée, astronomer and computer scientist, worked closely with Hynek as a mentee as he studied the UFO phenomenon. His proposed classification system offers four parent classifications with five subcategories that can be used with any of the parent classifications.

Vallée Classification System:

- **(CE)** Close Encounter – As described by Hynek.

- **(MA)** Maneuver – Craft makes an obvious deviation in direction during flight.

- **(FB)** Flyby – Craft flies in continuous line with no deviation.

- **(AN)** Anomaly – Unusual lights or unexplained entities involved with a craft.

Five subcategories which can be assigned to above classifications:

1. Sighting
2. Physical effects

3. Living entity or life form

4. Transformation of reality (witness loses time, disoriented, etc.)

5. Physiological impact including physical harm or death of animals/humans.

Class Name	1 Sighting	2 Physical Effect	3 Beings	4 Reality Transformation	5 Injury or Death
AN Anomaly	Amorphous lights, mystery explosions	Poltergeist, materialized objects, areas of flattened grass (i.e. crop circles)	Anomalies with entities (ghosts, yetis, cryptozoological beings, elves, spirits)	Near Death Experience (NDE), religious visions and miracles. Out Of Body Experience (OOBE)	Anomalous injuries or death, including spontaneous combustion and unexplained wounds
FB Flyby	Continuous trajectory	With physical evidence	Beings observed	Witness sense of reality change (such as landscape alteration, telepathy, etc)	Result of fly-by is injury or death
MA Maneuvers	Discontinuous trajectory	With physical evidence	Beings observed	Witness sense of reality change (such as landscape alteration, telepathy, etc)	Result of maneuver is injury or death
CE Close Encounter	Close approach (within 500')	With physical evidence	Beings observed	Abduction	Injury or death

Chapter 2: Abductee Narrative and Observations

These behaviors might be an indicator that someone is a potentially an abductee. Granted, one, a few, or even many of these is not a specific indication that they are in fact an abductee. When determining these potential factors from a witness do not read the list or ask if they have any of these indicators.

This information should only come from their testimony or you may essentially lead them to these conclusions based on their desire to be believed or fear that this information actually pertains to them when it may not.

Abductee Narrative

Thomas E. Bullard created a basic narrative of the abduction process through the collection of 270 purported alien abduction cases. In these narratives he found eight common ones as outlined below. Not all narratives will contain all of these examples nor will they necessarily be in this precise order.

- Capture – Abductee is taken, typically by force to a craft or testing area.

- Examination - These beings subject the witness to a physical and mental examination.Undressing the victim.
  - o Cleansing them.
  - o Examination by eyelike scanning device.
  - o Using tools to get specimens of skin, blood, and other fluids.
  - o Examining brain and reproductive system.
- Conference - A conversation with the beings follows.
- Tour - The beings show their captive around the ship.
- Otherworldly Journey - The ship flies the witness to some strange and unearthly place.
- Theophany - An encounter with a divine being occurs.
- Return - At last the witness comes back to Earth, leaves the ship, and reenters normal life.
- Aftermath - Physical, mental, and paranormal aftereffects continue in the wake of the abduction.

The above narrative was written by Sarah Andalaro and her article can be retrieved from:
http://visuastoriesufos.weebly.com/alien-abduction-narrative.html

For even more description of the abductee narrative:
https://en.wikipedia.org/wiki/Narrative_of_the_abduction_pheno menon

Abductee Observations

These behaviors might be an indicator that someone is a potentially an abductee. Granted, one, a few, or even many of these is not a specific indication that they are in fact an abductee. Again, when determining these potential factors from a witness do not read the list or ask if they have any of these indicators.

- Have had missing or lost time.
- Have been paralyzed in bed with a being in your room.
- Have unusual scars or marks with no possible explanation on how you received them.
- Have seen balls of light or flashes of light with no source.
- Have a memory of flying through the air that cannot be a dream.
- Have a strong "memory" that makes no sense but will not go away.
- Have seen beams of light outside your home or coming into your room from outside.
- Have many dreams of UFO's, beams of light or alien beings.
- Have had a shocking UFO sighting or multiple sightings.
- Have a strong sense of having a mission or important task to do without knowing where this compulsion comes from.
- Have had a false pregnancy or missing fetus.
- Have awakened in another place than where you went to sleep or don't remember going to sleep.
- Have had dreams of eyes looking at you or have a fear of eyes looking at you.
- Have awakened in the middle of the night, startled and feeling you are not alone.
- Have a strong reaction to pictures of aliens, either aversion or being drawn to them.
- Have inexplicably strong fears or phobias.
- Have had self-esteem problems most of your life.
- Have seen someone with you become paralyzed, motionless or frozen in time.
- Have a memory of a special place with spiritual significance when you were young.
- Have had someone in your life claim to witness a ship or

alien near you or witnessed you being missing.

- Have found blood or strange stains on your sheet or pillow with no explanation on how they got there.
- Have a compelling interest in UFO sightings or aliens.
- Have an extreme aversion towards the subject of UFO's or aliens.
- Have felt compelled to walk or drive to an unknown location or out of the way area.
- Have a feeling of being watched especially at night.
- Have had dreams of passing through windows or walls.
- Have seen a strange fog or haze that should not be there.
- Have heard strange humming or pulsing sounds and could not find a source.
- Have had unusual nosebleeds, or awakened with a nosebleed.
- Have awakened with soreness in your genitals which could not be explained.
- Have neck or back problems, or awaken with unusual stiffness in any part of your body.
- Have had chronic sinusitis or nasal problems.
- Have had electronics around you go haywire or oddly malfunction with no explanation.
- Have seen a hooded figure in or near your home.
- Have had frequent or sporadic ringing in your ears, especially in one ear.
- Have an unusual fear of doctors or medical treatment.
- Have insomnia.
- Have had dreams of doctors or medical treatments.
- Have frequent or sporadic headaches especially in the sinus, behind one eye or in one ear.
- Have a feeling that you are going crazy for thinking about these things.
- Have had paranormal or psychic experiences.
- Have been prone to compulsive or addictive behavior.
- Have channeled telepathic messages from aliens.
- Have heard an external voice in your head speaking to you.
- Have you been afraid of your closet?

- Have had sexual or relationship problems.
- Have to sleep "against" the wall or with your bed next to a wall.
- Have a feeling that you must be very vigilant or you may be taken away by someone.
- Have a very hard time trusting others.
- Have dreams of destruction or catastrophe.
- Have feelings that you are not supposed to talk about these things or must not.
- Have experienced many things in this list, and recall your children or parents speaking about similar experiences.
- Have tried to resolve these types of problems with little or no success.
- Have many of these traits but cannot remember anything about an alien abduction or alien encounter.

This list was compiled by the International Community for Alien Research (ICAR) and can be retrieved at:
http://icar1.homestead.com/abducteequestion.html

Chapter 3: Questionnaire Samples

The following samples questions are designed to be used as a supplement to the cognitive interview, but can also be used as telephone interview scripts. Granted, these samples could also be used as a personal interview and could even be submitted to a client to fill out if you feel the cognitive interview is not necessary or if you do not feel comfortable doing it. I highly recommend calling a witness as soon as possible after you receive their contact. A phone call immediately will not only help them remember details while they are fresh, assuming it's a recent sighting, but will also help thwart hoaxers who may be surprised by an actual phone call so quickly.

I have added some notes within the questions as further detail, guidance, as well as potential examples of what to expect or to help the client with marked within parentheses and in italics (*Note example*). By no means should you read these examples to the client unless absolutely necessary. The idea here is to get their vision of what they saw in their own words. By asking a client, "Can you describe the shape of the craft? Was it round, oval, oblong, or maybe cigar shaped?" you are leading the witness and limiting their answers as well as giving them certain answers that they feel you may be looking for. Ask the basic question, but allow them to paint the picture for you of what they saw and avoid putting descriptions out there to limit their vision.

These questions are also mostly formed as open ended questions. This means that the witness is free to describe things in their own words and is not limited to a yes/no answer. Avoid asking questions that only need a word or limited description to answer. Any question that merely needs a yes or no answer should be avoided unless it requires a specific answer, i.e., do you wear glasses?

The Mutual UFO Network website (http://www.mufon.com/) has a link on their site to report a UFO. The link opens up what they call their Case Management System. From here a witness will fill out their personal information along with a long series of questions and finally a narrative of what occurred.

The big issue I have with the MUFON online form is that a majority of the questions list specific answers and even though the witness has to make a selection I still feel it feeds how they should report their encounter. Another minor issue is that they ask the "what sized object would cover the UFO if you held it at arm's length?" question. I never ask this because people always seem to make it larger than what it would probably be. In their MUFON Field Investigator's Manual they specifically state to not use this as a method of measurement since people "vastly overestimate" the size when using this method (Sparks).

The MUFON Field Investigator's Manual does have some great forms at the end of the book. In addition to a general sighting case they also have electrical/magnetic, animal affect, psychological/physiological, landing traces/artifacts, entity, abduction, photographic, radar, residual radiation, animal mutilation, and aviation/pilot UFO Report forms. While these forms contain a lot of great questions they are essentially for the witness to fill out. And while these reports sound fantastic odds are pretty slim you might receive or even feel comfortable investigating some of these (mutilated animals?). If you do, however, most of these will more than likely need to involve an expert in a particular field to assist you with the investigation.

In addition to asking for a narrative I would ask these following questions if the information was not given to me prior. Granted, a properly conducted cognitive interview also allows you to explore these questions and in greater detail.

- What were you doing in the hours leading up to this event? (*Establish mood, awareness ability such as if they had just worked all day and went out afterward they may have been fatigued.*)
- What were you doing in the minutes and last seconds prior to the event? (*Establish location as well.*)
- What was the time and weather just prior to the event? (*Ask these together so they don't think too hard about the time. As far as the weather you want to know if they saw clouds, if it was precipitating, what direction the wind was coming from, and what the temperature was.*)
- Did it rain earlier in the day?
- What direction was the wind coming from relative to the direction you were standing?
- From where you were located what objects were between your eyes and the UFO?
- Could you see any other lights from where you first observed the UFO? (*This includes house lights, street lights, cars, the moon, everything!*)
- Did you notice anything else in the sky prior to, during, or after your sighting?
- How did you initially mentally process what you were seeing?
- As the event continued, how were you feeling emotionally?
- As the event unfolded how often did you look away? (*Did they glance down as they moved to get a better look, look down as they got their phone out of their pocket, go inside to get something?*)
- How did the UFO affect the environment it was in as it

moved? (*Affecting clouds or trees can give you an idea of elevation, distance, as well as speed.*)

- How did the object seem to move?

- How fast did the object seem to be moving?

- How far away do you feel the object was from you?

- How far away do you feel the object was from (closest large object the witness saw)? (*This will give us more information about the perceived distance since it is usually hard to accurately guess distances from us to other objects. Between these two estimates we can draw a better conclusion as to where the object might have been in conjunction with the following question*)

- When it moved did the UFO pass between you and any other object?

- How was the object shaped when you initially saw it? What about during the sighting?

- How bright did the object seem to you compared to other things you see at night? Did the object change brightness and did this seem to go with the direction of movement?

- From the direction you were standing where did the object go? (*Is this tied to the wind direction? This might not validate it as a Chinese lantern or balloon, but it could be a clue.*)

- In relation to the horizon how much higher was it compared to being completely overhead? (You could phrase this by splitting this up to between overhead and the horizon which was the UFO closest to? (*From there try and narrow it down especially using the actual scene once questions are finished.*)

- Did you feel the object reminded you of something recognizable? Not that this will explain it but just to relate to your experience.

- What time did the event end? (*Note I did not ask how long it lasted as the time start/stop forces them to put the encounter in perspective. You can always ask this question later and compare it to the time difference they give you although many times they will just assume based on how long they thought the event lasted.*)

- How did you feel once the event was over?
- What did you do then?
- Did you think of the event much after it happened?
- When did you first tell someone else about what you saw?
- How often have you retold the story? (*If they tell the story to too many people odds are that it may morph into something greater than what initially happened. If the first witness is someone they have not talked to about the incident more than it might be wise to ask them what the witness told them.*)
- Are you; colorblind? Hearing impaired?
- Were you; wearing glasses during or before the sighting? Under the influence of drugs, alcohol, or prescription medication?

Once these questions are completed it would be beneficial to ask the witness if they could show you the exact area where they saw the UFO. Even though you are asking questions specific to the scene of the event you would benefit more by asking them away from the site they witnessed the UFO. From there begin to document the scene through photographs.

Chapter 4: Further Information

The internet is full of information, and sometimes misinformation and you will easily find much more information out there than what I have collectively provided you here in this book. The following list is some resources to gather further information about many of the topics I briefly discussed in the book. Any link I referenced in the book will be found here with the exception of those found in other chapters in the resource section.

Obviously you could Google any topic, but these are my sites of choice although sometimes links suddenly expire with no warning. I have also included some further reading from books that I did not use as references, but will allow you to understand various aspects of this book in further depth.

- http://www.space.com/32054-satellite-tracker.html (live satellite tracker)
- http://www.spaceweather.com/flybys/ (satellite flybys by zip code)
- https://spotthestation.nasa.gov/sightings/ (satellite flybys by location)

- http://www.heavens-above.com/ (satellite tracker)
- http://www.stellarium.org/ (Historical star software)
- http://www.amsmeteors.org/ (American Meteor Society; up to date information on meteor showers and fireball sightings)
- https://www.wunderground.com/ (Current and historical weather information)
- https://sourceforge.net/projects/jpegsnoop/ (JPEGsnoop software for viewing EXIF and metadata of digital photographs)
- http://www.findexif.com/ (Place the URL of any photograph online to find the EXIF data)
- http://fotoforensics.com/ (Use URL or upload any photo for EXIF information or for basic analysis)
- https://digital-photography-school.com/ (Photography information)
- https://pipl.com/ (Conduct a basic background, photo, social media, and other information search on anyone based on name or email address)
- http://www.bbc.com/future/story/20170629-the-hidden-signs-that-can-reveal-if-a-photo-is-fake (Spotting fake photographs)
- http://rationalwiki.org/wiki/Pareidolia (Further information on pareidolia as well as examples)
- http://paranewsinsider.blogspot.com/2016/01/the-basics-of-researching-online-media.html (Or just go to ParaNewsInsider.com and click on the blog link at the top and then go to 2016 and then January- this blog post of mine discusses how to disseminate web stories for hoaxes
- https://www.ufoofinterest.org/ (UFO story researcher who exposes the truth about many UFO hoaxed photos/videos)
- https://www.metabunk.org (Website that rationally analyzes UFO, conspiracy, and paranormal stories)

- http://www.jimsdestinations.com/paraufo1.htm (Practical guide to becoming a UFO researcher/investigator)
- https://www.cia.gov/news-information/featured-story-archive/2016-featured-story-archive/how-to-investigate-a-flying-saucer.html (How to investigate UFOs from the CIA)
- https://www.cia.gov/library/center-for-the-study-of-intelligence/kent-csi/vol40no5/html/v40i5a09p.htm (CIA's role in the study of UFOs, 1947-1990)
- http://ancientaliensdebunked.com (*Ancient Aliens* television show debunked in a three hour video produced by Chris White and has commentary by Dr. Michael Heiser)
- http://www.cufon.org/cufon/afr200-2.htm (U.S. Air Force Regulation 200-2 (AFR 200-2) from August 12, 1954)
- https://tinyurl.com/yaaojxr5 (Example of anomalous research team's standards and protocols)
- http://readynutrition.com/resources/a-step-by-step-guide-for-how-to-make-a-kearny-fallout-meter_08082012/ (Instructions on creating a Kearny fallout meter)
- http://www.metaphysicsinstitute.org/ (Institute of Metaphysical Humanistic Science - Get Your Doctoral Degree in Paranormal Science, Parapsychology, Ufology, or Cryptozoology)
- http://www.tfuniversity.org/ (Thomas Francis University - Take Single Paranormal Courses or Get Your Bachelor's, Master's, and Doctoral Degree)

As previously mentioned the following books did not appear in this book as references, but I feel they should be ones that every serious researcher or investigator should read.

UFOs and Related Phenomena

Bullard, Thomas E. (2016). *The Myth and Mystery of UFOs*. Lawrence, Kansas. University Press of Kansas.

Costa, Cheryl, & Costa, Linda Miller. (2017). *UFO Sightings Desk Reference: United States of America 2001-2015*. Createspace.

Delgado, Pat, & Andrews, Colin. (1989). *Circular Evidence: A Detailed Investigation of the Flattened Swirled Crops Phenomenon*. Grand Rapids, Michigan. Phanes.

Graham, Robbie. (2017). *UFOs: Reframing the Debate*. White Crow Books.

Kitei, Lynne D. (2010). *The Phoenix Lights: A Skeptic's Discovery that We are Not Alone*. Charlottesville, Virginia. Hampton Roads Publishing Company.

Randle, Kevin D. (2000). *Scientific Ufology: Roswell and Beyond--How Scientific Methodology Can Prove the Reality of Ufos*. New York. HarperTorch.

Vallee, Jacques. (2014). *The Invisible College: What a Group of Scientists Has Discovered about UFO Influence on the Human Race*. San Antonio, Texas. Anomalist Books.

Verma, Surendra. (2004). *Why Aren't They Here? The Question of Life on Other Worlds*. London. Totem Books.

Interviewing/Body Language

Andersen, Peter A., Ph.D. (2004). *The Complete Idiot's Guide to Body Language*. New York. Apha Books.

Andersen, Peter A. Ph.D. (2007). *Nonverbal Communication: Forms and Functions, 2nd Edition*. Long Grove, Illinois. Waveland Press.

Dimitrius, Jo-Ellen, PhD. (1998). *Reading People: How to Understand People and Predict Their Behavior- Anytime, Anyplace*. New York. Random House.

Eckman, Paul. (2009). *Telling Lies: Clues to Deceit in the Marketplace, Politics, and Marriage*. New York. Norton.

Eckman, Paul. (2007). *Emotions Revealed: Recognizing Faces and Feelings to Improve Communication and Emotional Life, 2nd Edition*. New York. Holt Paperbacks, Macmillan.

Pease, Allan, & Pease, Barbara. (2004). *The Definitive Book of Body*

Language. New York. Bantam Dell.

Portigal, Steve. (2013). *Interviewing Users: How to Uncover Compelling Insights*. Brooklyn, New York. Rosenfeld Media.

Research

Gatum, Chris. (2016). The Beginner's Photography Guide, 2nd Edition. New York. DK.

Moche, Dinah L. (2014). Astronomy: A Self-Teaching Guide, Eighth Edition (Wiley Self Teaching Guides) 8th Edition. Hoboken, New Jersey. Wiley.

Moore, Sir Patrick. (2006). *Guide to Stars and Planets (Philip's Astronomy)*. Seattle, Washington. Philip's.

Investigation

Baker, Robert A., & Nickell, Joe. (1992). *Missing Pieces: How to Investigate Ghosts, UFOs, Psychics and other mysteries*. Buffalo, New York. Prometheus Books.

Federal Bureau of Investigation. (2015). *Handbook of Forensic Services*. Createspace.

Radford, Benjamin. (2010). *Scientific Paranormal Investigation: How to Solve Unexplained Mysteries*. Corrales, New Mexico. Rhombus Publishing.

Watson, Nigel. (2014). *UFO Investigations Manual: UFO investigations from 1982 to the present day*. Sparkford, England. Haynes.

Miscellaneous

Chabris, Christopher, & Simmons, Daniel. (2010). *The Invisible Gorilla: And Other Ways Our Intuitions Deceive Us*. New York. Crown Publishing.

Shaw, Dr. Julia. (2016). *The Memory Illusion: Remembering, Forgetting, and the Science of False Memory*. London. Random House Books.

Chapter 5: References

Abramson, Alana. (2017, March 15). *A Google Balloon Crashed in This Country and People Thought It Was a UFO*. Retrieved from: http://fortune.com/2017/03/15/google-balloon-ufo-colombia/

Alvear, Cecillia. (2005, July 5). *Martians take Quito, or so we thought*. Retrieved from: http://www.today.com/id/8472909/ns/today-today_entertainment/t/martians-take-quito-or-so-we-thought/#.WJ5iXm_yuM8

Andrews, Colin. (2009). *Dedication to my dear friend and co-author, Pat Delgado*. Retrieved from: http://www.colinandrews.net/Research-Dedication-PatDelgado.html

Appleyard, Bryan. (2005). *Aliens: Why They are Here*. London. Scribner.

Basterfield, Keith. (2013, May 28). *"Fairy rings" and Delphos*. Retrieved from: http://ufosscientificresearch.blogspot.com/2013/05/fairy-rings-and-delphos.html

Bohannon, John. (2015, December 21). Eyewitness testimony may only be credible under these circumstances. *Science Magazine.* Retrieved from: http://www.sciencemag.org/news/2015/12/eyewitness-testimony-may-only-be-credible-under-these-circumstances

Birnes, William J. (2004). *The UFO Magazine UFO Encyclopedia.* New York. Pocket Books.

Byrd, Deborah. (2016, November 9). *Why stars twinkle, but planets don't.* Retrieved from: http://earthsky.org/space/why-dont-planets-twinkle-as-stars-do

Casey, Michael. (2015, March 20). *Hummingbird, thought extinct, rediscovered in Colombia.* Retrieved from: http://www.cbsnews.com/news/hummingbird-rediscovered-after-nearly-70-years-in-colombia/

Colavito, Tony. (2012, May 21). *The Soviet Search for Ancient Astronauts.* Retrieved from: http://www.jasoncolavito.com/blog/the-soviet-search-for-ancient-astronauts

Craddock, Tony. (1997-2000). *List of Possible UFO/ET Craft Crashes and Retrievals.* Retrieved from: http://www.cseti.org/crashes/crash.htm

Cuoghi, Diego. *Art and UFOs? No Thanks, Only Art.* Retrieved from: http://www.bibliotecapleyades.net/ufoart/UFOArt2/arteufo.htm

Dahlgreen, Will. (2015, September 28). *You are not alone: most people believe that aliens exist.* Retrieved from: https://today.yougov.com/news/2015/09/28/you-are-not-alone-most-people-believe-aliens-exist/

Danelek, J. Allan. (2008). *UFO's: The Great Debate.* Woodbury, Minnesota. Llewellyn Publications.

DiBlasio, Natalie. (2012, June 26). *A third of Earthlings believe in UFOs, would befriend aliens.* Retrieved from: http://usatoday30.usatoday.com/news/nation/story/2012-06-26/ufo-survey/55843742/1

Dicklow, M. Bess. (2011, August). *Fairy Ring and Localized Dry Spot.* Retrieved from: https://ag.umass.edu/turf/fact-sheets/fairy-ring-localized-dry-spot

Dohrer, Elizabeth. (2012, September 25). *Laika the Dog & the First Animals in Space.* Retrieved from: http://www.space.com/17764-laika-first-animals-in-space.html

Duran, Frank. *Snippy the Horse - the Most Famous Horse in the World!* Retrieved from: http://www.snippy.com/

Fowle, Zach. (2008, April 22). *Phoenix man: Neighbor caused Monday's mysterious lights.* Retrieved from: http://archive.azcentral.com/community/phoenix/articles/2008/04/22/20080422abrk-strangelights0422.html

Friedman, Stanton, MSc. (2008). *Flying Saucers and Science.* Franklin Lakes, New Jersey. New Page Books.

Gabbert, Bill. (2015, December 31). *Update on the legality of sky lanterns — banned in 29 states.* Retrieved from: http://wildfiretoday.com/2015/12/31/update-on-the-legality-of-sky-lanterns-banned-in-28-states/

Geiselman, Edward R., & Fisher, Ronald P. (2014). *Interviewing Witnesses and Victims.* Retrieved from: https://www.psych.ucla.edu/sites/default/files/documents/other/Current_CI_Research.docx

Geraghty, Paul. (2012, October 22). *Doug and Dave: The Crop Circle Hoaxers.* Retrieved from: http://www.spookystuff.co.uk/douganddavethecropcirclehoaxers.html

Glenday, Craig. (1999). *The UFO Investigator's Handbook.* Philadelphia. Running Press.

Goode, Erich. (2012). *The Paranormal: Who Believes, Why They Believe, and Why it Matters.* New York. Prometheus Books.

Gordon, Stan. (2010). *Silent Invasion: The Pennsylvania UFO-Bigfoot Casebook.* Greensburg, Pennsylvania. Stan Gordon Productions.

Gosling, John. *War of the Worlds Invasion: the Historical Perspective.* Retrieved from: http://www.war-ofthe-worlds.co.uk/war_worlds_quito.htm

Gregory, R.L, & Zangwill, O. L. (1963). The origin of the autokinetic effect. *Quarterly Journal of Experimental Psychology, 15*(4). Retrieved from: http://www.tandfonline.com/doi/abs/10.1080/174702163 08416334?journalCode=pqje19

Grinnell, R. (2016). Group Polarization. *Psych Central.* Retrieved from https://psychcentral.com/encyclopedia/group-polarization/

Haines, Gerald K. (2007, May 8). *CIA's Role in the Study of UFOs, 1947-90.* Retrieved from: https://www.cia.gov/library/center-for-the-study-of-intelligence/kent-csi/vol40no5/html/v40i5a09p.htm

Hasse, Joel. (2015, November 14). *Betty and Barney Hill Abduction.* Retrieved from: http://fourthkind.com/betty-and-barney-hill/

Hedges, Kathleen. (2010, March 4). *Charles B. Moore, 1920-2010: New Mexico Tech Notes Passing of Noted Atmospheric Researcher.* Retrieved from: http://www.nmt.edu/news/3704-charles-b-moore-1920-2010

Heussner, Ki Mae. (2010, April 26). *Stephen Hawking: Alien Contact Could Be Risky.* Retrieved from: http://abcnews.go.com/Technology/Space/stephen-hawking-alien-contact-risky/story?id=10478157

Hickman, Leo. (2010, April 26). *Stephen Hawking takes a hard line on aliens.* Retrieved from: https://www.theguardian.com/commentisfree/2010/apr/2 6/stephen-hawking-issues-warning-on-aliens

Hill, Sharon. (2016, January 10). *Nothing interesting happens in Canberra, eh? UFO hoax revealed (and it's deemed 'not interesting').* Retrieved from: http://doubtfulnews.com/2016/01/nothing-interesting-happens-in-canberra-eh-ufo-hoax-revealed-and-its-deemed-not-interesting/

Innocence Project. (2017). *DNA Exonerations in the United States.* Retrieved from: https://www.innocenceproject.org/dna-exonerations-in-the-united-states/

Johnson, Jeffrey K. (2012). *Super-History: Comic Book Superheroes and American Society, 1938 to the Present.* Jefferson, North Carolina. McFarland & Company.

Kean, Leslie. (2009, November 11). *The Conclusion of the NASA Lawsuit: Concerning the Kecksburg, PA UFO case of 1965.* Retrieved from: http://www.theufochronicles.com/2009/11/conclusion-of-nasa-lawsuit-concerning_10.html

Koi, Isaac. *Koi UFO Video 070: F14B Tomcat / UFO Recovery ("The Orion Conspiracy").* Retrieved from: http://www.isaackoi.com/ufo-videos/koi-ufo-video-070.html

Kraska, Jake. (2015, August 3). *The Psychology of Comic Books: Why We Worship Superheroes.* Retrieved from: http://www.lateralmag.com/articles/issue-1/i-need-a-hero-why-were-wired-to-worship-superheroes

Lickerman, Alex, M.D. (2011, April 24). *The Two Kinds of Belief: Why infants reason better than adults.* Retrieved from: https://www.psychologytoday.com/blog/happiness-in-world/201104/the-two-kinds-belief

Lindell, Jeffery A. (1991). *Interviews with Harold Augspurger, Commander 415th Night Fighter Squadron; Frederic Ringwald, S-2 Intelligence Officer, 415th Night Fighter Squadron.*

Lorgen, Eve Francis, M.A. (1998, April 3). *Alien Implant Removals: Before and After Effects.* Retrieved from:

http://www.mufon.com/alien-implants/alien-implant-removals-before-and-after-effects

Majors, Dan. (2015, December 6). Five decades later, the Kecksburg UFO is identified (probably). *Pittsburgh Post-Gazette*. Retrieved from: http://www.post-gazette.com/news/science/2015/12/06/50-years-later-the-Kecksburg-Westmoreland-County-UFO-is-identified-probably/stories/201512060146

McAndrew, James. (1994). *The Roswell Report: Fact vs. Fiction in the New Mexico Desert*. Washington, D.C.: Headquarters United States Air Force.

McAndrew, James. (1997). *The Roswell Report: Case Closed*. Washington, D.C.: Headquarters United States Air Force.

McGaha, James, & Nickell, Joe. (2015). *Alien Lights? At Phoenix, Stephenville, and Elsewhere: A Postmortem*. Retrieved from: http://www.csicop.org/si/show/alien_lights_at_phoenix_stephenville_and_elsewhere_a_postmortem

Miller, David L. (2013).*Introduction to Collective Behavior and Collective Action: Third Edition*. Long Grove, Illinois. Waveland Press.

Mori, Kentaro. (2012, April 8). *Erich von Daniken: Fraud, Lies and Bananas*. Retrieved from: http://forgetomori.com/2012/aliens/erich-von-daniken-fraud-lies-and-bananas/

Mowing-devil. Retrieved from: https://en.wikipedia.org/wiki/Mowing-Devil

Naisbitt, Michael. (2008, February 29). *The Sun - Thames UFO & London Eye UFO Identified? (Feb 2008)*. Retrieved from: http://blog.ufo-blog.com/2008/02/sun-thames-ufo-london-eye-ufo.html

New World Encyclopedia. (2009, May 10). *Autokinesis*. Retrieved from: http://www.newworldencyclopedia.org/p/index.php?title=Autokinesis&oldid=941884

Nicholson, Malcolm. (2013). *UFOs, Cultural Tracking and Science Fiction* (first published in *Ufologist*, Vol. 16, No. 5, January-February 2013). Retrieved from: https://malcolmnicholson.wordpress.com/ufos-cultural-tracking-and-science-fiction/

Nickell, Joe. (2001). *Real-Life X-Files: Investigating the Paranormal*. Lexington, Kentucky: The University Press of Kentucky.

Paris, Antonio. (2017). *The "Wow!" Signal*. Retrieved from: http://planetary-science.org/research/the-wow-signal/

Parsons, Brian. (2015, November 30). *#UFOSA #BUSTED Cape Town Green UFO Hoax*. Retrieved from: http://paranewsinsider.blogspot.com/2015/11/ufosa-busted-cape-town-green-ufo-hoax.html

Perkins, Forrest D. (1968, February 13). *Letter from T/Sgt. Forrest Perkins to the University of Colorado Condon Committee*. (Correct transcript of handwritten letter prepared by Brad C. Sparks 30 Dec 79). Retrieved from: http://martinshough.com/aerialphenomena/Lakenheath/Perkins1.htm

Pflock, Karl T. (2001). *Roswell: Inconvenient Facts and the Will to Believe*. Buffalo, New York: Prometheus Books.

Pooley, Jefferson, & Socolow, Michael J. (2013, October 28). *The Myth of the War of the Worlds Panic*. Retrieved from: http://www.slate.com/articles/arts/history/2013/10/orson_welles_war_of_the_worlds_panic_myth_the_infamous_radio_broadcast_did.html

Project Blue Book - *Unidentified Flying Objects*. (2016, August 15). National Archives and Records Administration. Retrieved from: https://www.archives.gov/research/military/air-force/ufos.html

Radford, Benjamin. (2008, April 23). *Mysterious Phoenix Lights a UFO Hoax*. Retrieved from: http://www.livescience.com/2483-mysterious-phoenix-lights-ufo-hoax.html

Radford, Benjamin. (2011a). *Tracking the Chupacabra: The Vampire Beast in Fact, Fiction and Folklore*. Albuquerque, New Mexico. University of New Mexico Press.

Radford, Benjamin. (2011b, February 11). *Hoax in the Holy Land: Jerusalem UFO a Proven Fake*. Retrieved from: http://www.livescience.com/12826-jerusalem-ufo-hoax.html

Radford, Benjamin. (2014). *Mysterious New Mexico: Miracles, Magic, and Monsters in the Land of Enchantment*. Albuquerque, New Mexico. University of New Mexico Press.

Randle, Kevin D., & Rodeghier, Mark. (2002). Frank Kaufmann Reconsidered. *International UFO Reporter (IUR)*. (Fall 2002). (8-26). Retrieved from: http://www.cufos.org/FrankKaufmannExposed.pdf

Randle, Kevin D. (2007, September 15). *How Did Frank Kaufmann Slip Through?* Retrieved from: http://kevinrandle.blogspot.com/2007/09/how-did-frank-kaufmann-slip-through.html

Rao, Joe. (2016, March 18). *How to Spot Satellites*. Retrieved from: http://www.space.com/6870-spot-satellites.html

Redfern, Nick. (2015*). Secret History: Conspiracies from Ancient Aliens to the New World Order*. Detroit, Michigan. Visible Ink Press.

Rojas, Alejandro. (2014, April 1). *Virgin's UFO prank frightens police on April Fools' Day in 1989*. Retrieved from: http://www.openminds.tv/virgins-ufo-prank-frightens-police-april-fools-day-1989/26742

Ruhl, Dick. (1976). *A History of APRO*. Retrieved from: https://web.archive.org/web/20080524071220/http://mimufon.org/1970%20articles/Apro_History.htm

Sagan, Carl. (1968, July 29). *Symposium on Unidentified Flying Objects: Hearings Before the Committee on Science and Astronautics U.S. House of Representatives Nineteenth Congress Second Session, July 29, 1968*. Internet Edition Prepared by National Capital Area Skeptics (NCAS). Retrieved from: http://files.ncas.org/ufosymposium/sagan.html

Seaburn, Paul. (2017, June 30). *Russian Satellite Will Be Brighter Than Stars and Planets*. Retrieved from: http://mysteriousuniverse.org/2017/06/russian-satellite-will-be-brighter-than-stars-and-planets/

Scherker, Amanda. (2013, August 30). *Alabama Residents Panic After Radio Station's Joke Alien Invasion*. Retrieved from: http://www.huffingtonpost.com/2013/08/30/alabama-radio-alien-invasion_n_3844715.html

Schuessler, John F. (2013). *A Brief History of MUFON*. Retrieved from: http://www.mufon.com/history.html

Sherif, Muzafer. (1935). A study of some social factors in perception: Chapter 2. *Archives of Psychology*, 1935, 27, No. 187, 17-22. Retrieved from: https://brocku.ca/MeadProject/Sherif/Sherif_1935a/Sherif_1935a_2.html

Smallwood, Karl. (2016, March 29). *The Story Behind the Crop Circle Phenomenon*. Retrieved from: http://www.todayifoundout.com/index.php/2016/03/two-men-started-phenomenon-crop-circles-planks-wire/

Sparks, Brad. (2008). Basic Elements of UFO Data – Time, Location, Duration, Angular Size. *MUFON Field Investigator's Manual*, 115-125.

Spencer, John. (1991). *The UFO Encyclopedia*. London: Headline.

Stacy, Dennis. (1985). *Close Encounter with Dr. J. Allen Hynek*. Retrieved from: http://paul.rutgers.edu/~mcgrew/ufo/hynek-interview

Switek, Brian (1992). The Idiocy, Fabrications and Lies of Ancient Aliens. *Smithsonian Magazine*. Retrieved from: http://www.smithsonianmag.com/science-nature/the-idiocy-fabrications-and-lies-of-ancient-aliens-86294030/

Talbott, Nancy. (2012, April 14). *Non-local Communication & a "Time" Aberration as Pat Delgado & Dave Chorley Images Appear on Video & Digital Cameras*. Retrieved from: http://www.bltresearch.com/robbert/delgadochorley.php

Taylor, Richard. (2011, August 1). *Physics could be behind the secrets of crop-circle artists*. Retrieved from: http://www.iop.org/news/11/aug/page_51614.html

The Numbers. *All Time Worldwide Box Office*. Retrieved from: http://www.the-numbers.com/box-office-records/worldwide/all-movies/cumulative/all-time

United States Air Force. (1954). *Project Blue Book Special Report #14*. Retrieved from: https://archive.org/details/ProjectBlueBookSpecialReport14

University of New Hampshire (UNH). *Guide to the Betty and Barney Hill Papers, 1961-2006*. Retrieved from: http://www.library.unh.edu/find/archives/collections/betty-and-barney-hill-papers-1961-2006

Vallance, Tom. (1999, March 19). Obituary: Stefan Schnabel. *The Independent*. Retrieved from: http://www.independent.co.uk/arts-entertainment/obituary-stefan-schnabel-1082825.html

Ventre, John. (2015a). Was Kecksburg UFO a GE Mark 2 Reentry Vehicle? *MUFON UFO Journal, December 2015*. Retrieved from: http://www.mufon.com/ufo-news/has-a-top-5-ufo-case-been-solved

Ventre, John. (2015b). *Case for UFOs*. Charlottesville, Virginia. Lang Publications.

Westcott, Kathryn. (2013, July 1). *Five problems caused by Chinese lanterns*. Retrieved from: http://www.bbc.com/news/magazine-23129276

Wikipedia contributors. (2017, June 16). *Identification studies of UFOs*. Retrieved from: https://en.wikipedia.org/wiki/Identification_studies_of_UFOs

Wixted, John, & Mickles, Laura. (2017, June 13). *Eyewitness Memory Is a Lot More Reliable Than You Think: What law enforcement, and the public, needs to know*. Retrieved from: https://www.scientificamerican.com/article/eyewitness-memory-is-a-lot-more-reliable-than-you-think/?WT.mc_id=SA_TW_MB_NEWS&sf88225189=1

Wolchover, Natalie. (2012, May 11). *The Surprising Origin of Alien Abduction Stories*. Retrieved from: http://www.livescience.com/20250-alien-abductions-origins.html

Brian can be contacted at Brian@BrianDParsons.com and be sure to listen to the *Paranormal News Insider* radio show live every Tuesday night at 7 PM eastern at http://wcjvradio.com or visit http://paranewsinsider.com for archive information (or find the show on your favorite app).